Michael J. Petrie
Jan 5, 1994

D0561010

A dic · tion · ar · y *of* LITURGICAL TERMS

A
dic·tion·ar·y
of LITURGICAL
TERMS

Philip H. Pfatteicher

Trinity Press International
Philadelphia

First Published 1991

Trinity Press International
3725 Chestnut Street
Philadelphia, PA 19104

Interior design: CREATION

Printed in the United States of America

Library of Congress Cataloging-in-Publication Data

Pfatteicher, Philip H.
    A dictionary of liturgical terms/Philip H. Pfatteicher.
       p.   cm.
    ISBN 1-56338-026-9:
    1. Liturgics—Dictionaries. I. Title.
BV173.P42 1991
264'.003--dc20   91-22075
                                    CIP

To

Carolyn and Thomas

and

Sarah and Robert

in *Hochzeitliche* celebration

Preface

This dictionary is a concise glossary of words used in talking about liturgy and worship. Within its scope fall the various parts of the liturgy of Christianity, the names of various liturgical books, the vestments of the ministers and the altar, the architecture and ornaments of the building, titles of various ministers. The scope is deliberately wide—East and West, Catholic and Protestant, Europe and America—reflecting the breadth and depth of present liturgical studies. For the study of liturgy leads one inevitably into learning the names of the various parts and uses of the historic liturgy inherited by the present church from apostolic times and from Judaism before that, enriched through centuries of adaptation, discovery, and growth, and then beyond the texts of the liturgy into a vast variety of fields of human knowledge. In the liturgy one finds a distillation of the fullness of human experience.

Compilers of glossaries and dictionaries, beginning with Samuel Johnson, have often allowed themselves the privilege of indulging, with less restraint than elsewhere, their crotchets, prejudices, and idiosyncratic opinions. This not only affords the compiler an opportunity for a kind of wry release but provides the reader, in addition to instruction, entertainment as well. Dr. Johnson's *Dictionary* (1755) is a surprisingly pleasant compendium of knowledge and opinion. His definitions of oats ("A grain, which in England is generally given to horses, but in Scotland supports the people"), of pension ("An allowance made to anyone without an equivalent. In England it is generally understood to mean pay given to a state heirling for treason to his country"), of Tory ("One who adheres to the ancient constitution of the state, and the apostolical hierarchy of the church of England, opposed to a Whig"), and of Whig ("The name of a faction") are well known. The "harmless drudge" (Dr. Johnson's definition of lexicographer) who is the compiler of this glossary has attempted to maintain that tradition of singularity, and here and there gives vent to certain prejudices which he nonetheless believes are held on good authority and stand on solid ground.

Pronunciations are given, even of relatively simple words, to prevent avoidable embarrassing errors—the compiler having heard a graduate student in theology speak of a HOR-i-zon, a pretentious art critic refer to de-COR-a-tive sculpture, a bored guide to a great church make reference to a pec-TOR-al cross.

Derivations of the words glossed in this book are provided as assistance in understanding the words and also as a way of suggesting how the liturgy is intertwined with the history of the English language. Old English dates from the Anglo-Saxon invasion of England, around 450, to 1200; Middle English from around 1200 to 1500; Modern English from the beginning of the sixteenth century. Etymology is simplified here, and several steps in the derivation of words are often omitted. For example, French frequently stands between Middle English and Latin, Latin between Middle English and Greek, medieval Latin between English and classical Latin.

This dictionary, because of the limitations of the compiler, emphasizes the Western church, especially the Lutheran, Anglican, and Roman Catholic traditions as they occur in North America. The liturgical terms of the Eastern church are represented to a limited degree. Certain terms from Jewish liturgy as it has influenced Christian worship are also to be found in these pages.

Certain architectural terms helpful in talking about liturgical matters are included in this book. Those symbols encountered in church architecture and decoration are also included, although the study of symbols is a very large field of its own and often requires illustrations.

Words in SMALL CAPITALS are glossed in their alphabetical place, and the reader is referred to those locations for further information.

Books and compilations useful in gathering the terms included in this book and making the definitions have included Paul Zeller Strodach's glossary in his *Manual on Worship*, rev. ed. (Philadelphia: Muhlenberg Press, 1946); George R. Seltzer's glossary in Luther D. Reed's *The Lutheran Liturgy* (Philadelphia: Muhlenberg Press, 1947, 1960); Edward N. West's glossary in *Church Buildings and Furnishings*, ed. Jonathan G. Sherman (Greenwich, CT: Seabury Press, 1958); J. S. Purvis, *Dictionary of Ecclesiastical Terms* (London and New York: Thomas Nelson and Sons, 1962). I have previously prepared glossaries for the *Manual on the Liturgy*, which I wrote with Carlos Messerli (Minneapolis: Augsburg Publishing House, 1979), and my *Commentary on the Occasional Services*

(Philadelphia: Fortress Press, 1983). Three recent studies are Jovian Lang, *Dictionary of the Liturgy* (Boynton Beach, FL: Franciscan Fathers, 1990); Charles M. Guilbert, *Words of Our Worship* (New York: Church Hymnal Corporation, 1990); and Michael Sansom, comp., *A Liturgical Glossary,* Grove Liturgical Study, no. 42 (Bramcote, Nottingham, England: Grove Books Ltd., 1985). Users of this glossary who desire more extended studies than those included here are directed to Frank L. Cross, ed., *The Oxford Dictionary of the Christian Church*, 2d ed. (New York: Oxford University Press, 1974); University of America staff, *New Catholic Encyclopedia*, 17 vols. (1967; reprint, Palatine, IL: Publishers Guild, 1981); J. G. Davies, ed., *The New Westminster Dictionary of Liturgy and Worship* (Philadelphia: Westminster Press, 1986); and Peter E. Fink, ed., *The New Dictionary of Sacramental Worship* (Collegeville: Liturgical Press, 1990).

In the following pages, when mention is made of the *Book of Common Prayer*, unless otherwise noted, it is the American Prayer Book of 1979 that is intended, although that book has much in common with its many predecessor books.

The Lutheran family of books includes the following. *The Church Book* is the liturgy and hymnal published by the authority of the General Council of the Evangelical Lutheran Church in America in 1868 with several subsequent editions. *The Common Service Book* is the book authorized and published by the United Lutheran Church in America in 1917 with a slightly revised second edition in 1918 and a text edition in 1919. *The Service Book and Hymnal* is the book authorized by the Lutheran churches in North America, cooperating in the Commission on the Liturgy and Hymnal, that came by merger to be two: the American Lutheran Church and the Lutheran Church in America (the book was published in 1958). *The Lutheran Book of Worship* was prepared by the churches participating in the Inter-Lutheran Commission on Worship (the Lutheran Church in America, the American Lutheran Church, the Evangelical Lutheran Church of Canada, and the Lutheran Church—Missouri Synod; the first two bodies merged to form the Evangelical Lutheran Church in America, the third became the Evangelical Lutheran Church in Canada). The book was published in 1978. The Ministers' Edition contains the complete liturgical text; the pew edition contains those portions of the liturgy needed by the congregation, together with the hymnal.

A cappella (ah ca-PELL-ah; Italian, in the manner of the chapel). Choral music sung without accompaniment.

Aaronic benediction (a-RON-ik). The blessing commanded in Numbers 6:22-27, given to Moses by God, to give to Aaron and his descendents to bless the Israelites. It is much beloved by Lutherans, regarded as the only blessing commanded in Scripture and suggested by Luther to have been the blessing given by Christ to the apostles as he ascended into heaven. It appears three times in the *Lutheran Book of Worship* (at the close of the Service of the Word, at the close of ante-communion, and as an alternative at the close of the Eucharist); it appears in the *Book of Common Prayer* at the close of An Order of Worship for the Evening and at the Commital for the Burial of the Dead.

Abbot (AB-ett; Old English from Aramaic *abba*, father). The title of the head of certain independent religious orders such as the Benedictines. In the Middle Ages the pope frequently honored certain abbots of prominent monasteries with permission to wear the MITER and RING and to carry a CROZIER.

Ablution (ab-LOO-shun; Middle English from Latin *abluere*, to wash away). The ceremonial rinsing of the CHALICE after the communion. The cleansing was originally done after the service in the SACRISTY, but in the tenth or eleventh century it was introduced into the structure of the mass in part as a testimony to the real presence of Christ in the Sacrament.

Absolution (Middle English from Latin *absolvere*, to set free from). The declaration, traditionally reserved to ordained ministers of the church, of the forgiveness and the wiping away of sins. Absolution is found in three forms in Christianity: the **indicative** form, "I absolve you"; the **(de)precatory** form, in which the confessor prays for the forgiveness of the penitent, such as "May almighty God have mercy on you, forgive you all your sins, and bring you to everlasting life"; and the **declaratory** form, a statement or declaration of grace that God forgives the penitent, such as "In the mercy of almighty God, Jesus Christ was given to die for you, and for his sake God forgives you all your sins."

1

Abstinence (Middle English from Latin *abstinere*, to abstain). Doing without something (for example, meat) as an act of devotion on certain days such as Good Friday and the other Fridays in Lent. See FAST.

Acclamations. The **Gospel acclamations** are congregational bursts of praise before ("Glory to you, O Lord") and after ("Praise to you, O Christ") the Gospel in the Holy Communion as an acknowledgment of the presence of Christ, who speaks in the Gospel reading. The **eucharistic acclamations** are the congregation's responses during the eucharistic prayer, such as "Christ has died, Christ is risen, Christ will come again."

Acolyte (AK-a-light; Middle English from Greek *akolytos*, one who follows). Originally one of the minor orders of ministry; later the term was used to denote one who carried a torch or a CANDLE in a liturgical procession, and then was applied to any layperson who serves by preparing the altar and assisting the ministers of the services of the church.

Address. See ALLOCUTION.

Adiaphora (ah-dee-AFF-or-ah; Greek, indifferent [the singular is *adiaphoron*]). A word originating in Greek Stoic philosophy to describe conditions over which one could exercise no control, as opposed to actions with moral significance which could be described as good or evil. The term was revived at the time of the Reformation to describe "ceremonies and church rites which are neither commanded nor forbidden in the Word of God but which have been introduced into the church with good intentions for the sake of good order and decorum" (*Formula of Concord* X.1). Adiaphora aroused controversy during the seventeenth century and have seldom if ever been the neutral matter the name implies.

Administration (Middle English from Latin *administrare*, to render service to). The distribution of the elements of the Holy Communion to the communicants.

Advent (Middle English from Latin *advenire*, to come to). 1. The preparatory and anticipatory season beginning four Sundays before Christmas and lasting until Christmas Eve. 2. The incarnation of Christ. 3. The second advent, the glorious appearing of Christ as judge on the last day.

Advent wreath. A circle of evergreen set with four candles, one of which is lighted on the first Sunday in Advent, two on the second Sunday, three on the third, and four on the fourth Sunday, suggesting the increasing anticipation of the light of Christ that will fill the world with unending life. The custom originated among German Lutherans and has spread widely through Christianity.

Affusion (Latin *affusio*, a pouring upon). The pouring of the water of Holy Baptism over the candidate's head rather than IM-MERSION or SUBMERSION of the candidate in the water. Affusion began to replace immersion in about the eighth century in the West.

Agape (ah-GAH-pay; Greek, love). A love feast in the early church, closely related to the Eucharist, at which offerings to the poor were gathered. It became corrupted with abuses (1 Corinthians 2:17-34) and was forbidden by the Council of Carthage in 397.

Agenda (ah-JEN-da; Latin plural of *agendum*, German *Agende*, things to be done). A book containing the services and offices of the church, primarily for use by the clergy. The term has been so used since the fourth century, but is seldom used in this sense in English except in certain Lutheran quarters.

Agnus Dei (AHG-noose DAY-ee; Latin, Lamb of God). 1. An ancient hymn to Christ, the Lamb of God, based on John 1:29 (also Isaiah 53:7 and Revelation 5:6ff.), sung at the breaking of the bread in the Eucharist or during the communion or at other times, as in the Litany. The Agnus Dei appears twice in the American *Book of Common Prayer* (1979): in the Great Litany (p. 152) and in the Holy Eucharist Rite I (p. 337), both times in the older Tudor translation. In the *Lutheran Book of Worship* there are two forms of the canticle: "Jesus, Lamb of God" (Canticle 1) and "Lamb of God" printed in the text of the

Holy Communion, intended by the International Commission on English Texts, which prepared both translations, to be repeated as often as necessary to accompany the breaking of the bread. 2. A symbol of Christ as a lamb, seated or standing, carrying over its shoulder a cross-topped staff with a PENNON (a flag ending in two points) bearing a red cross. The lamb has a triradiant NIMBUS (a halo with wedge-shaped rays forming the top three arms of a cross).

Aisle (Middle English from Old French *aile*, Latin *ala*, wing). A part of a church divided laterally from the NAVE and parallel to it, bounded by columns, piers, or walls; hence the common phrase "center aisle" is technically meaningless; properly, the space between successive rows of chairs or pews is called an **alley**.

Alb (Middle English from Latin *alba*, white). A narrow-sleeved, ankle-length, close-fitting white garment, worn at the services of the church by all ranks of ministers, ordained and unordained. The classical tunic, an everyday garment, became a specifically church vestment in the fifth century. The traditional prayer while vesting associates the alb with purification through the blood of the Lamb of God (Revelation 7:14): "Cleanse (*dealba*) me, Lord, and purify my heart, that being made white in the blood of the Lamb, I may have the fruition of everlasting joys."

Alenu (a-LAY-new; Hebrew, "It is incumbent upon us [to praise]"). A sublime prayer found near the end of all Jewish services, originating probably in the third century of the Common Era, combining praise of the oneness of God with the selection of Israel as God's people.

Alexandrine rite (al-ex-ANN-drin). The LITURGY OF ST. MARK in Greek, the parent of all other Egyptian liturgies. After Chalcedon (541), the Melchites alone used the Liturgy of St. Mark, and the Copts and Ethiopians modified it in Coptic and Ge'ez. The rise in importance of Constantinople led to the displacement of the Liturgy of St. Mark by the BYZANTINE liturgy, and by the twelfth century the Liturgy of St. Mark had disappeared.

Alignment or **Alinement** (French *aligner* from Latin *a*, to, *ligne*, a line). The arrangement of ministers at the altar. In the medieval period the place of the deacon was immediately behind the celebrant on the step below the FOOTPACE where the priest stood, that of the subdeacon immediately behind the deacon on the step below him; whenever the celebrant turned toward the people, the subdeacon knelt. The preferred alignment in present practice is for the deacon to stand to the presiding minister's right and the subdeacon to the left so that they may more conveniently assist in the celebration.

All Hallows. See ALL SAINTS' DAY.

All Saints' Day. November 1. Also called **All Hallows**. Originally a feast in honor of all the martyrs, dating from the fifth century in the East, the celebration was expanded during the eighth century to include all the saints, even those who were not martyrs. At the time of the Reformation, the New Testament understanding of "saint" as including all believers was recovered, and the feast became a celebration of the unbroken unity of the whole church, living and dead. The collect for the feast in the *Book of Common Prayer* and borrowed by the Lutheran rite declares, "Almighty God, whose people are knit together in one holy Church, the body of Christ our Lord, grant us grace to follow your blessed saints. . . ." We living saints follow those saints now in the blessedness of heaven.

All Souls' Day. November 2. A solemn memorial day for the departed Christians who were not exemplary saints or martyrs or confessors, first kept in 998. In the present Roman calendar, the day is called the Commemoration of All the Faithful Departed. In view of their expanded understanding of ALL SAINTS' DAY, the Anglican and Lutheran churches have generally found this day an unnecessary duplication.

Alleluia (Greek form of the Hebrew *Hallelujah*, praise the Lord). The song of heaven and the Easter shout of gladness and victory used in the Holy Communion to greet and welcome the Gospel, and often added to songs and chants of Easter. During the Middle Ages, alleluia was personified and treated almost as a living creature, buried with mourning before Lent began and resurrected with ceremony and great rejoicing at Easter.

Alleluia dulce carmen (DOOL-chay CAR-men). A Latin hymn applying Psalm 137 to the situation of the church facing the Lenten exile in the wilderness, first found in manuscripts of the eleventh century, sung at the putting away or "burial" of ALLELUIA. The hymn is best known in English in John Mason Neale's translation, "Alleluia, song of sweetness,/Voice of joy that cannot die."

Alley. See AISLE.

Allocution (al-low-CUE-shun; Latin *ad loqui*, to speak to). A brief, formal address to the congregation as in the address to the sponsors in Holy Baptism, to advise or instruct. In the Swedish liturgy of 1811, the opening address is called The Allocution.

Alma Redemptoris mater. (AHL-ma re-DEMP-tor-iss MAH-tair; Latin, loving mother of the Redeemer [gate of heaven, star of the sea, assist your people who have fallen . . .]). One of the four antiphons to the Virgin Mary (the others are *AVE, REGINA caelorum, REGINA COELI,* and *SALVE, REGINA*) sung to conclude Compline (or

otherwise to conclude the daily office) from Advent through the Presentation (February 2), ascribed to Hermannus Contractus (1013-1054). Originally sung as an antiphon to a psalm or canticle and now used as an independent anthem. In the present Liturgy of the Hours, the antiphon may be used at any time of the year.

Alms (Middle English from Greek *eleemosune*, pity). Money or goods given in charity to the poor.

Alms basin or **bason.** 1. A dish in which the money offerings of the people are gathered. 2. A large plate on which the offering plates are received from the ushers by a server or minister. The spelling "bason" in Lutheran use is a borrowing from a variant spelling of "basin," common in the Anglican church, on the assumption that it must be the proper style.

Almuce (AL-myoos; Latin *almuta*). A fur-lined hood or cape with long ends hanging down in front; worn in certain religious orders.

Alpha and omega. The first and last letters of the Greek alphabet used as a symbol for Christ, based on Revelation 1:8.

Altar (Old English from Latin *altare*, to burn up [sacrificial offerings], and *altus*, high place). The holy table on which the Lord's Supper is celebrated; the central furnishing of a church building, symbolic of the meeting of God and the congregation;

the place of God's action and of the people's offering of themselves in response. The altar is usually embellished with all the gifts which art, skill, and love can contribute and is vested with cloths, frequently but not necessarily in the seasonal color, and the FAIR LINEN. Some modern altars are not intended to be vested (the principal statement by color therefore being made by the presiding minister's chasuble), but the altar should always be covered with the fair linen. The altar, as the principal focus of the building and the center of eucharistic action, should never be overshadowed by a large or life-sized cross suspended above or behind it.

Altar of repose. In Western use, an altar other than the HIGH ALTAR, decked with flowers and many candles, on which the Sacrament rests following the Maundy Thursday evening Eucharist, and before which a watch is kept in preparation for the communion on Good Friday. The practice is first mentioned in the fifteenth century.

Altar rail. A railing across or enclosing the SANCTUARY at which communicants kneel. In certain neo-Gothic churches there is an additional rail, the **chancel rail**, a low partition, that separates the chancel from the nave.

Alternative Service Book. A book produced by the Church of England in 1980 as an alternative, rather than a replacement, for the 1662 *Book of Common Prayer*, in large measure because the established church could reform the Prayer Book only with parliamentary approval.

Ambo (AM-bo; Latin from Greek *ambon*, a raised edge, rim). A platform approached by a flight of steps and surrounded by a parapet from which the lessons were read and litanies conducted in a Christian BASILICA. In some later churches the ambo is one of a pair.

Ambrosian (Am-BRO-sian). Pertaining to the USE of Milan, the see of St. Ambrose; a rite of the Western church, separate from the use of Rome and still in existence.

Ambry. See AUMBRY.

Ambulatory (AM-bue-la-tory; Latin *ambulare*, to walk). A processional passageway around the back of the high altar.

Amen (Ah-MEN; Hebrew, firm, sure, trustworthy; translated by Luther, "Yes, it shall be so"). An expression of confidence that God hears the prayers of his people, said by the congregation to give assent to a prayer spoken by another. (Cf. Deuteronomy 27:15-26; Psalm 106:48; Matthew 6:13; Romans 16:27; Revelation 3:14; 22:20, 21.) See also GREAT AMEN.

Amice (AM-iss; Middle English from Latin *amicire*, to wrap around). A rectangular collar of white linen placed over the head to form a hood which, after the other vestments are put on, is dropped back as a collar. The amice is often omitted with modern albs having attached collars. The traditional prayer while vesting connects it with the helmet of salvation (Ephesians 6:17): "Lord, put the helmet of salvation on my head that I may overcome the assaults of the devil." The amice is not to be confused with the ALMUCE.

Ampulla (am-PULL-eh, Latin). A ceremonial vessel used to contain the oil of anointing.

Amyss. Another name for an ALMUCE.

Anamnesis (usually, especially in English use, a-NAM-na-sis; or in Greek, a-nam-NAY-sis, remembrance). An act by which a person or event is made ritually present. Specifically, it is the church's response to Jesus' command "Do this in remembrance of me" (Luke 22:19; 1 Corinthians 11:24), and is that portion of the GREAT THANKSGIVING which recalls the whole life and work of Christ, making those saving deeds a contemporary experience. By the anamnesis, the promise (Gospel) inherent in the remembered event is celebrated as the central reality in the faith and life of the Christian community.

Anaphora (an-AFF-or-a; Greek, carry up, offering). THE GREAT THANKSGIVING, beginning with the PREFACE versicles and concluding with the GREAT AMEN.

Anchor. A symbol of Christian hope, deriving from Hebrews 6:19.

Andrew. See APOSTLES' SYMBOLS.

Angels (Middle English from Greek *angelos*, messenger). Bodiless, non-corporeal, immortal created beings attendant upon God. In pseudo-Dionysus the Areopagite and medieval angelology, there were nine ranks of celestial beings arranged in three orders of three choirs each, angels being the lowest: seraphim, cherubim, thrones; dominations (dominions), virtues, powers; principalities (princedoms), archangels, angels. Their names are derived from Isaiah 6:2 (seraphim), Ezekiel 10:16 etc. (cherubim), Jude 9 and 1 Thessalonians 4:16 (archangels), and especially in the Vulgate translation, Ephesians 1:21 (*supra omnem principatum, et potestatem, et vertutem, et dominationem*) and Colossians 1:16 (*sive throni, sive dominationes, sive principatus, sive potestates*). Of the archangels, St. Michael (September 29) has been venerated since early times; the 1969 Roman calendar extends this day to include St. Gabriel and St. Raphael. The Lutheran and Anglican calendars extend it to include all the angels of whatever rank. The Holy Guardian Angels are commemorated on the Roman calendar on October 2, a feast which first appeared in the sixteenth century.

Angelus (ANN-jell-us; Latin, angel). 1. A devotion in commemoration of the incarnation, consisting of three scriptural verses ("The angel declared unto Mary, and she conceived of the Holy Spirit; 'Behold, the handmaid of the Lord; be it unto me according to your word'; The word was made flesh and dwelt among us"), each followed by AVE MARIA; a collect (that is used in the Lutheran and Anglican rites on the ANNUNCIATION); and a blessing. 2. The bell rung at morning, noon, and sunset to accompany the devotion.

Anglican chant. A chant formula in four-part harmony designed for successive verses of psalms and CANTICLES. It is an English Reformation era adaptation of Gregorian chant and continental harmonized chant. A single chant serves one verse with a division at midpoint; a double chant serves a pair of verses.

Announcement of the church year. A custom that developed in the early Middle Ages before calendars were easily available. Following the reading of the Gospel on the EPIPHANY, January 6, the dates of the major events of the remainder of the church year were solemnly announced (SEPTUAGESIMA, ASH WEDNESDAY, EASTER, ASCENSION, PENTECOST, and the first Sunday in ADVENT), thus binding the concluding Christmas cycle to its fulfillment in the Easter cycle as parts of one whole proclamation. The custom continued into the twentieth century in Roman Catholic monasteries and cathedrals and was revived in many Lutheran congregations.

Annunciation (a-NUN-see-A-shun; Middle English from Latin *annuntiare*, to make known). The celebration on March 25 of the announcement by the archangel St. Gabriel to the Blessed Virgin Mary that she was to be the mother of the Savior. The commemoration of the beginning of the incarnation from which the years have been reckoned, March 25 was until the eighteenth century observed as New Year's Day.

Ante-communion (Latin *ante*, before). The service of the Holy Communion up to the OFFERTORY, especially when used as a separate service. Sometimes called the pro-anaphora; sometimes derisively called a DRY MASS.

Antependium (ann-tee-PEND-ee-um; Latin, hanging before). The vestment, usually but not necessarily in the color of the season, which "hangs before," that is, on the front of the altar; the frontal.

Anthem (Middle English from Latin *antiphona*, sung responses). A quasi-liturgical choral composition usually based on Scripture. It is specified in Anglican services (in which it can also mean verses that may be read), but it does not form part of the Roman or Lutheran liturgy, although it is often added to Lutheran services.

Antidoron (AN-tee DOOR-on; Greek, instc ͻd of the gift). In the Byzantine rite, the blessed bread, being what remains of the loaves from which the eucharistic bread is cut, distributed to the congregation after the eucharistic liturgy or after the reception of Holy Communion. Also called the EU-LOGY.

Antiminsion (AN-tee MINN-see-on; Greek, instead of a table). In the Eastern church, a silk or linen cloth decorated with representations of the passion and especially the entombment of Christ, containing relics; originally used as a portable altar, now always used even on consecrated altars.

Antiochene rite (an-tee-OKK-een). The rite of Antioch (Syria), with Alexandria and Rome comprising the three great patriarchates of the ancient church. See EASTERN LITURGIES.

Antiphon (ANN-ti-fonn; Greek *antiphonos*, sung responses, from *anti*, opposite, and *phone*, voice, voice opposite voice). A verse, usually from Scripture, sung before and after and sometimes interspersing the verses of a psalm or canticle to draw out a particular theme or to relate the psalm or CANTICLE to the day or season.

Antiphonal psalmody (an-TIFF-on-al). The division of chants between two different voices or groups of voices. The antiphonal psalmody in the mass is the INTROIT (entrance psalm), OFFER-TORY, and COMMUNION verse. See RESPONSORIAL PSALMODY.

Antiphonary. A book containing the ANTIPHONAL PSALMODY for a season or for the church year.

Apostles' Creed. The baptismal statement of faith dating in its present form from about 500 and traceable to the Roman SYMBOL (baptismal formula) of the second century. The name implies that this creed summarizes the apostolic teaching of the CATHOLIC church. A pleasant tradition, no older than the fourth century, describes the creed as the spontaneous composition of the twelve apostles, each apostle contributing a phrase.

Apostles' Days. The festivals commemorating the twelve apostles, Matthias (or Paul) replacing Judas Iscariot. As in the Gospel lists, the apostles are celebrated sometimes singly, sometimes in pairs: Andrew (November 30), Bartholomew (August 24), James the Greater (July 25), John (December 27), Peter and Paul (June 29), Philip and James the Less (May 1), Matthew (September 21), Matthias (February 24), Simon and Jude (October 28), Thomas (December 21).

Apostles' symbols. Among others, the most commonly used are these: **Andrew**, a saltire (X-shaped) cross, signifying, according to a late medieval tradition, his crucifixion on a cross of this shape; **Bartholomew**, three flaying knives, the instruments of his death; **James the Elder,** three scallop shells, representing his pilgrimages to establish Christianity in Spain; **James the Less,** a saw to indicate that he was thus dismembered in his martyrdom; **John**, a serpent in a chalice, because his enemies tried unsuccessfully to poison him; **Judas**, thirty pieces of silver and a rope, indicating his treachery and suicide; **Jude**, a ship, because of his missionary journey to King Abgarus of Edessa; **Matthew**, three money bags, because he had been a tax collector; **Matthias**, an open Bible and a double-headed axe, because he was chosen by lot to replace Judas in the number of the Twelve and became a martyr by being beheaded; **Paul**, a sword, because he was beheaded, sometimes shown also with an open book marked *Spiritus gladius*, the sword of the Spirit (Ephesians 6:17); **Peter**, two crossed keys, sometimes one of gold and one of silver, recalling the gift of the keys of heaven to bind and to loose sinners (Matthew 16:19); **Philip**, a Latin cross with a loaf of bread on either side, indicating his crucifixion and his remark at the feeding of the five thousand (John 6:7); **Simon**, a book with a fish resting on top of it, to show that he became a fisher for people (Matthew 4:19) by the power of the word of God; **Thomas**, a spear behind a carpenter's square, showing his trade as a builder (tradition says he built a church with his own hands in India) and the instrument of his death.

Apostolic Constitutions. A CHURCH ORDER dating from ca. 360-380, the most extensive liturgical and canonical compilation of the ancient church, generally thought to be of Syrian provenance, making use of documents already in existence. The book has had limited influence, in part because it betrays Arian leanings and was condemned at the Council of Trullo (691-692).

Apostolic Tradition. A work of Hippolytus of ca. 215, containing detailed descriptions of rites and practices at Rome in the later second century. The identification of the anonymous treatise, in the nineteenth century given the name *The Egyptian Church Order*, as a work of Hippolytus was established in the first quarter of the twentieth century.

Apparel (Middle English from Old French *apareillier*, to prepare). A decorative strip of material applied to any vestment, frontal, or hanging. Most commonly, apparels are worn on the outside of the AMICE, like a standing collar, and on the sleeves of the ALB at the cuffs and on the middle of the skirt of the alb, just above the hem, back and front. They need not be in the liturgical colors but may be of any color that complements the vestments.

Applique (app-li-KAY; French from Latin *applicare*, to apply). A decoration or ornament usually embroidered, cut out and applied to a PARAMENT or vestment.

Apse (APPS; Latin *apsis* [*absis*], arch, vault). A semicircular or multiangular termination of a church building, especially the altar or EAST end of a church.

Archangels. See ANGELS.

Archbishop (Old English from Greek *arkhiepiskopos*, archbishop). In the fourth or fifth century the title was applied to PATRIARCHS and other holders of important sees; it was later extended to METROPOLITANS and PRIMATES holding jurisdiction over an ecclesiastical PROVINCE.

Archdeacon. A cleric, now, despite the name, usually a priest, having administrative authority delegated by the bishop in the whole or part of the diocese. A dean. Originally the chief of the deacons.

Archimandrite (ar-ki-MAN-drite; Greek, ruler of a fold, from *mandra*, monastery). A title in use in the Eastern church since the fourth century, originally the superior of a monastery or several monasteries, the equivalent of the Western ABBOT; now a title given to distinguished celibate priests, ranking below a bishop.

Archpriest (Middle English). 1. From the fifth century, the senior presbyter of a city, assisting the bishop; later the ARCHDEACON took over the administrative responsibilities and the archpriest performed liturgical duties in the absence of the bishop. 2. A RURAL DEAN. 3. In the Orthodox church a title of honor, the highest rank to which a married priest can attain.

Ark (Old English from Latin *arca*, a chest, box). 1. The cabinet in a synagogue in which the scrolls of the Torah are kept, deriving from the Ark of the Covenant described in Exodus 25:10-16. 2. The boat built by Noah for survival during the flood (Genesis 6-9), and hence a symbol for the church, offering safety and hope in a dying world (1 Peter 3:18-21). Sometimes the symbol is a ship with a sail, bearing a cross or a monogram of Christ.

Ascension (Middle English from Latin *ascendere*, to ascend). The celebration, on the fortieth day of Easter, of the last of the resurrection appearances of the risen Christ and his reception and coronation in heaven.

Ascription (Middle English from Latin *ascribere*, to add to in writing). A statement attributing praise to God, such as the GLORIA PATRI. An ascription is sometimes made at the conclusion of a sermon, especially in Anglican churches, with such words as "And now to God the Father, God the Son, and God the Holy Spirit, be all honor and glory, both now and forever."

Ash Wednesday. The most solemn day of the church year, commemorating the fall of humanity into sin (Genesis 3) and each individual's share in that rebellion; the beginning of LENT, the forty weekdays before EASTER.

Ashes (Old English). A sign of mortality and of cleansing, used anciently as a sign of mourning and used in Christianity on **Ash Wednesday** to begin the Great Fast. The ashes are made from the palms of the previous PASSION (Palm) SUNDAY.

Asperges (ass-PER-jeez; Latin *aspergere*, "to sprinkle"; *asperges me*, "You will wash me [with hyssop]" from Psalm 51). The ceremonial purification of the church and the congregation by sprinkling with blessed water with an ASPERGILIUM or, in the Eastern church, an ASPERSORIUM. The action recalls baptism and is done as a preparatory rite before the entrance hymn, especially during LENT and the days of EASTER. The rite consists of Psalm 51 with verse 7 as an ANTIPHON, versicles, and a collect; during Easter the Psalm is 117 with Vidi Aquam ("I saw water flowing from the right side of the temple, and all to whom that water came were saved, and they shall say: alleluia, alleluia") as the antiphon.

Aspergilium (as-per-GILL-ee-um; Latin, sprinkler). A short metal rod with a sponge enclosed in one end used to sprinkle blessed water; also called an ASPERSORIUM.

Aspersorium (as-per-SORE-ee-um; Latin *aspergere*, to sprinkle). 1. A small broom made of dried plants used especially in the Eastern church to sprinkle blessed water. 2. A vessel for holding blessed water; a STOUP.

Aspiciens a longe (a-SPIK-ee-aynes a LONG-gay; Latin, watching from afar [I see the power of God advancing]). The magnificent RESPONSORY used at Matins (now the Office of Readings) on the first Sunday in Advent, made familiar to English-speaking Christians by its use in the Festival of Lessons and Carols at King's College, Cambridge, on Christmas Eve.

Ass, Feast of the (*Eselfest*). A mock festival, observed in medieval France and Germany on the feast of the Circumcision (January 1) or on the octave of the Epiphany (January 13), celebrating the donkey on which Mary had come to Bethlehem, which had worshiped at the manger, and which carried Mary and the infant Jesus into Egypt to escape Herod. The custom is first recorded at Rouen in the tenth century and continued as late as 1634 in Sens. The hymn tune *Orientis partibus* covered the procession of a woman and child on a donkey through the town and into the church.

Assisting minister. The name in the *Lutheran Book of Worship* for an ordained or lay person who assists the presiding minister by performing such tasks as reading lessons, leading certain prayers, preparing the altar at the offertory, distributing Holy Communion.

Assumption (a-SUM-shun; Middle English from Latin *assumptio*, a taking up). The commemoration on August 15 of the death of the Virgin Mary, her "Falling Asleep" or **Dormition** as it is known in the Eastern church, and her **Departure** (another name for the feast) to heaven. The feast has its origins in the fifth century in Jerusalem. The title "Mary's Assumption" dates from the seventh century in Gaul; the doctrine asserts that upon her death, Mary was assumed body and soul into heaven as a precursor of all the faithful.

Asterisk. See STAR COVER.

Athanasian Creed (Ath-an-ASIAN). A profession of faith used in the Western church, known by its opening words, *Quicunque vult*. Its traditional attribution to Athanasius, Bishop of Alexandria, who died in 373 (the Council of Autun in 670 refers to it as "The faith of St. Athanasius") seems inaccurate, and the symbol probably originated in Gaul in the fourth or fifth century.

Atrium (AY-tree-um). The court in front of a basilica, often cloistered on all four sides.

Attende caelum (a-TEN-day KYE-lum). "Give ear to what I say, you heavens," a Song of Moses selected from Deuteronomy 32(:1-4, 7, 36a, 43a) that in the *Lutheran Book of Worship* is sung following the eleventh lesson in the Easter Vigil and that may be used at other times such as the Old Testament canticle in Morning Prayer. In the Roman Catholic Liturgy of the Hours, the canticle is Deuteronomy 32:1-12 and is used as the Old Testament canticle on Saturday of Week II at Morning Prayer.

Audite coeli (au-DEE-tay CHAY-lee). Canticle 10 in the *Common Service Book* and in the *Service Book and Hymnal*, from Deuteronomy 32(:1-4, 9, 36, 40, 43.) See *ATTENDE CAELUM*.

Aumbry or **ambry** (AHM-bree; Middle English from Latin *armarium*, a cupboard, safe). A wall cabinet or safe in which the consecrated elements of the Holy Communion are reserved for distribution to the sick and the oils blessed by the bishop are kept. In the medieval period the aumbry was a more general recess or cabinet in which sacred vessels, books, and vestments were kept. See SACRAMENT HOUSE.

Aurora mass (a-ROAR-a; Latin, dawn). The mass of Christmas dawn, celebrated in Rome at the Church of St. Anastasia.

Ave Maria (Latin, Hail, Mary). The angelic salutation, an ascription of praise to the Blessed Virgin Mary based on the greetings of the archangel Gabriel (Luke 1:28) and Elizabeth (1:42). The use of the biblical verses dates from the eleventh century. The added verses, "Holy Mary, Mother of

God, pray for us sinners now and at the hour of our death," came into general use in the sixteenth century, being included in the Roman Breviary of 1568. The Ave Maria was deleted from the Roman office in 1955.

Ave maris stella (MAR-iss STELL-a; Latin, Hail, star of the sea). A rhythmical hymn to Mary dating at least from the ninth century, attributed to various authors, among them Paul the Deacon (ca. 720-800).

Ave regina (re-GEE-na; Latin, Hail, queen of the heavens). One of the four antiphons to the Virgin Mary sung to conclude daily prayer, first found in the twelfth century. In the Roman Breviary it was sung after Compline from the Presentation (February 2) through Wednesday in Holy Week; in the Liturgy of the Hours it may be used at any season. See *ALMA REDEMPTORIS MATER*.

Baculum (BAK-you-lum; Latin, a stick, staff). The Latin name for the hooked-top scepter, the ancient symbol of authority, which ultimately came to be used by Christian bishops.

Baldichino (ball-di-KEE-no), **Baldachin** (BALL-di-chin), **Baldaquin** (BALL-di-kin; from Italian *Baldacco*, Baghdad, from whence came rich cloth). A canopy of fabric hung over an altar as a sign of honor; also called a **tester**. When the canopy is made of wood, stone, or metal and rests on four columns, it is correctly called a **ciborium**.

Bands. Two strips of linen worn in front of the collar of a black gown (*Talar*) by clergy, particularly in Switzerland, Germany, England, and Scotland and in Roman Catholic churches in France and Spain. The bands or *Beffchen* are a remnant of the ruff collar worn in the sixteenth and seventeenth centuries by nobility and professional classes and served as the only clerical collar there was before the latter part of the nineteenth century. See CLERICAL DRESS.

Bangor antiphonary. The only surviving liturgical authority for the choir office in the Celtic church, written in an Irish monastery at Bangor between 680 and 691.

Banners. Flags adorned with sacred symbols for use in processions and for display in churches. Banners derive from ancient warfare and may be understood to suggest spiritual combat.

Banns (Middle English *banes*, to proclaim). The notice of the intention to marry given publicly in the church in which the ceremony is to take place in order that prayer may be made for the couple and that any who have objections, particularly legal impediments, to the marriage may make the objections known before the day of the wedding.

Baptisand (bap-tiz-AND; Latin *baptizandus*, gerundive of *baptizare*, to baptize). A seldom-used name for a candidate for Holy Baptism.

Baptism of Christ. The commemoration of the baptism of Jesus in the Jordan River by John, celebrated in Lutheran and Episcopal churches on the first Sunday after the Epiphany, in the Roman Catholic church in the United States the day following the Epiphany (which is observed on Sunday).

Baptist(e)ry (BAP-tis-tree; Middle English, from Greek *baptisterion*, a bathing place). 1. The building or area of a building which surrounds the baptismal font; the space where Holy Baptism is administered. 2. A large pool-sized font for baptism by immersion.

Bartholomew See APOSTLES' SYMBOLS.

Basilica (ba-SILL-i-ka; Latin, from Greek *basilike*, royal portico, court). 1. An early type of church building derived from the Roman hall used for legal or business purposes; the basilica is rectangular with an APSE at one end, columns extending the length of the NAVE, and a NARTHEX or arcaded porch at the other end. 2. A title of honor in the Roman Catholic church bestowed by the pope on certain important churches. There are four great patriarchal basilicas in Rome: St. John Lateran, the cathedral of the diocese of Rome; St. Peter's in the Vatican; St. Paul's outside the Walls; and Santa Maria Maggiore (St. Mary Major). These, together with three others—St. Laurence outside the Walls, Holy Cross in Jerusalem, and St. Sebastian—comprise the "seven churches of Rome."

Basilican posture. The presiding minister at the Holy Communion facing the congregation across the altar; employed in the first churches built under Constantine in the form of a modified BASILICA with the altar in the WEST end, away from the wall, allowing the bishop and presbyters to preside from behind it, facing east. In the middle of the fourth century that arrangement was reversed so that the altar was at the EAST end so the congregation could face east. Eventually the clergy moved to the west side of the altar so as to face the same way as the people, and the altar was moved toward the wall of the APSE to give more space. In the last third of the twentieth century, altars were again moved away from the east wall so that the ministers could stand behind them and preside at the Eucharist in the basilican manner.

Bay (Middle English from Old French *baer*, to gape). An integrated division of the side of a building, determined by structural components such as arches, columns, or piers.

Beans, blessing of. See BLESSING OF BEANS.

Beating the bounds. A procession on the ROGATION DAYS around the boundaries of the parish while singing the Litany, hymns, and psalms, and making a STATION at various landmarks. The custom makes sense only in territorial parishes.

Bees. 1. A general symbol of cooperation and industry. 2. A symbol of self-sacrificing labor, the bees giving of themselves to provide the wax for candles. 3. Because bees were anciently thought to arise spontaneously, their origin was understood to be parthenogenic, and thus they came to be associated with the Blessed Virgin Mary, showing her virginal maternity.

Beffchen. See BANDS.

Belfry (BELL-free; Middle English *berfrey*, a tower). A tower or steeple, or that part of a tower or steeple in which one or more bells are hung.

Bell (Old English). Bells have been used in Christian worship at least since the time of Gregory of Tours (ca. 585); since the eighth century they have been blessed by a bishop with holy water and CHRISM, probably owing to their ability to speak a language of praise and devotion, which raised them above dumb nature and made them partake of a human characteristic. In the BYZANTINE RITE, bells are attached to the chains of the CENSER to stimulate the auditory as well as the olfactory and visual senses; bells are also attached to the vestments of bishops in imitation of the high priest of ancient Israel.

Bell, Passing. A bell rung at the time of death to notify the parish of the passing of one of its members so that prayer could be offered for the person making the transition from this world to the next.

Bell, Sanctus. A bell rung at the singing of the SANCTUS in the Eucharist to enhance the solemnity of the angelic hymn and to rouse the congregation's attention to the heart of the GREAT THANKSGIVING. It eventually gave way to the ringing of the bell at the ELEVATION and before the communion of the priest, in which case it is called a **sacring bell**.

Bema (BAY-ma; Greek, platform). The raised platform or "holy place" which constituted the SANCTUARY in early churches. In later Eastern churches it is enclosed by the ICONOSTASIS or screen, which is ornamented with icons of the saints.

Benedicamus Domino (ben-eh-dik-AH-mus DOM-in-oh). Latin, "Let us bless the Lord," to which the response is, "Thanks be to God" (*Deo gratias*). This verse and response was used anciently to conclude each of the offices of daily prayer and mass; after it no further benediction was said.

Benedicite Omnia Opera (Ben-eh-DEE-chi-tay OM-ni-a O-per-ah). Latin, "All you works of the Lord, bless the Lord," a song of creation, called the Song of the Three Young Men or the Song of the Three Children in the fiery furnace, given in the additions to Daniel 3 in the Apocrypha (vss. 35-65). In the *Lutheran Book of Worship*, it is sung following the last lesson in the Easter Vigil during the procession to the font and may be used at other times, such as at Morning Prayer as the Old Testament canticle, as it is in the *Book of Common Prayer*, especially appropriate during Easter.

In the Lutheran book, in addition to appearing in the text of the Easter Vigil, it is given as Canticle 18. In the American *Book of Common Prayer* (1979), the song appears as Canticle 1 in Morning Prayer, Rite I, and in a modern translation as Canticle 12 in Morning Prayer, Rite II. In the Roman Catholic Liturgy of the Hours, the canticle is used at Morning Prayer on Sunday in Weeks I and III.

Benediction (Middle English from Latin *benedicere*, to bless). 1. Imparting God's blessing upon God's people at the close of a service. The use of such a blessing was not general until the later Middle Ages. Blessings occur in two forms: declarative and precatory. Declarative blessings include the benediction given in the *Lutheran Book of Worship* at the conclusion of Holy Communion and of Corporate Confession and Forgiveness ("Almighty God, Father, Son, and Holy Spirit, bless you now and forever") and a variant at the conclusion of the preaching office added to Morning and Evening Prayer; the benediction given in the *Book of Common Prayer* at the close of the Holy Eucharist, Rite I ("The blessing of God Almighty, the Father, the Son, and the Holy Spirit, be upon you and remain with you for ever"). Precatory blessings include the benediction given in the *Book of Common Prayer* at the close of Compline and daily devotions for families ("The almighty and merciful Lord, Father, Son, and Holy Spirit, bless us and keep us"); the benediction given in the *Lutheran Book of Worship* at the close of Morning Prayer, with a variant at the close of Responsive Prayer 1 ("The Lord almighty bless us, and direct our days and our deeds in his peace"). 2. A devotional office before the Blessed Sacrament, culminating in the blessing of the congregation with a consecrated host held in a MONSTRANCE. The origin of this practice dates from the eleventh century.

Benedictional. In the Western church, a book containing the texts of blessings imparted by the bishop during mass, after the Lord's Prayer, and before the KISS OF PEACE (*Pax domini sit semper vobiscum*). The oldest extant copy dates from the seventh century.

Benedictus [Dominus Deus] (ben-ay-DIK-tuss). Latin, "Blessed be the Lord, the God of Israel," the song of Zechariah from Luke 1:68-79, since ancient times appointed as the Gospel canticle at Morning Prayer (Lauds), in part because of its reference to "the dawn from on high."

Benedictus es, Domine, Deus Israel. Latin, "Blessed be thou, Lord God of Israel," a song of David (1 Chronicles 29:10-18) given as Canticle 12 in the Lutheran *Service Book and Hymnal* (1958); in the Roman Liturgy of the Hours, it is the canticle at

Morning Prayer on Monday of Week I.

Benedictus es, Domine, [Deus patrum nostrorum]. Latin, "Blessed are you, Lord," the Song of the Three Young Men from the additions to Daniel 3 (vss. 29-34), given as Canticle 2 and Canticle 13 in Morning Prayer in the *Book of Common Prayer* and in the Roman Liturgy of the Hours as the canticle at Morning Prayer on Sunday of Weeks II and IV. See BENEDICITE OMNIA OPERA.

Benedictus qui venit. Latin, "Blessed is he who comes [in the name of the Lord]," the concluding verse of the Sanctus in the Eucharist, based on Matthew 21:9 and added to the **Sanctus** in the fifth century. Retained universally in Lutheran rites, it became a matter of controversy among Anglicans because to some it contradicted a Calvinist interpretation of the Holy Communion as the spiritual rather than the physical presence of Christ in the Sacrament.

Berakah (ber-ah-KAH; Hebrew, blessing, plural *berakoth*). The characteristic Jewish prayer form which blesses God, recounting with thanksgiving his acts of mercy to his creation (Genesis 24:27; Job 1:21; Psalm 28:6; 2 Corinthians 1:3; 1 Peter 1:3).

Bergamo sacramentary (bear-GAH-mo). One of the two surviving representatives of a sacramentary of the Ambrosian rite, the ninth-century *Sacramentarium Bergonense.*

Bidding prayer. A form of prayer in which a deacon or assisting minister bids (invites) the people to pray for a particular request; silence for private prayer follows, and the people's prayers are summed up in a collect by the presiding minister, which the people confirm by their AMEN. The bidding prayer is one of the oldest forms of prayer in the church's treasury, dating from the *APOSTOLIC CONSTITUTIONS* (ca. 380); because of its antiquity, it has always been part of the Good Friday liturgy.

Bier (Old English, to bear, carry). The framework trestle on which a coffin is placed during a funeral.

Bination (by-NAY-shun; Latin *bini*, two by two). The celebration of two masses in one day by the same minister. The practice is forbidden in the Orthodox church and is possible in the Roman church only with dispensation; other churches are less scrupulous.

Biretta (bir-ET-ta; Latin *birretum*, cap). A square cap with three or four stiff ridges and a pompon in the center, worn by clergy. It is black for priests, purple for bishops, and red for cardinals. *Berretta* is the Italian name for one of the developments of the medieval cap which, being made of four pieces, was the common parent of the academic "mortarboard" (which developed through a hardening of the top surface), the "square cap" (a hardening of the four sides of the cap), and the biretta (a hardening of the upper seams of the cap). The biretta declined in use in the later twentieth century and is now not generally worn inside a church. In the Eastern church, archpriests and priests, for distinguished service, receive a black pointed cap (*skufya*) or a black cylindrical hat (*kalimavkion* or *kamilavkion*).

Birkat ha-mazon. The berakah or thanksgiving after a meal in Jewish practice, closely related to the prayers in the *Didache* 10 and the development of the Great Thanksgiving.

Birkat yotser. A "doorway of praise" which, in the Jewish liturgy, leads to the profession of the SHEMA. It begins with praise of the Creator of light and darkness and continues with praise of God who created the angels and the SANCTUS. The *Birkat yotser* may have served as a model for the Christian ANAPHORA.

Bishop (Old English form of Latin *episcopus*, from Greek, overseer, guardian). A church superintendent or overseer who has particular charge of the pastors and congregations within a particular area. The chief pastor of a diocese who is assisted in ministry by the presbyters.

Bittgaenge (BIT-geng-eh). German term for processions with litanies on ROGATION DAYS.

Black. A liturgical color of mourning, formerly used in the Roman rite for funerals and in Lutheran practice on Good Friday. The present Roman rite has curtailed its use, and the Lutheran rite suggests its use only on Ash Wednesday.

Black-letter Days. An Anglican term for those recognized saints' days for which the Prayer Book provided no special propers; these lesser saints' days were printed in black in calendar listings in the Prayer Book, as distinct from major feasts printed in red.

Black rubric or Declaration on Kneeling. A rubric printed in black because it was added at the last minute while the book was in process of being printed; black rubrics follow the rubrics printed in red at the conclusion of the service of Holy Communion in the 1552 *Book of Common Prayer* in response to pressure brought by John Knox and others, declaring that to receive communion kneeling did not mean that "any adoracioun" was thereby done to "anye reall and essential presence ... of Christ's naturall fleshe and bloude" and that it is against the truth of Christ's natural body "to be in moe places than in one, at one tyme." The controversial rubric was deleted in the 1559 Prayer Book, but was restored in a revised form in the 1662 book.

Blessing (Old English). The authoritative pronunciation of sanctity or the invocation of divine favor. See BENEDICTION.

Blessing of beans. New beans were blessed at the Ascension Day mass in certain places during the Middle Ages as a continuation of ancient fertility and harvest festivals. The blessing was done just before the *per quem haec omnia* of the canon of the mass.

Blessing of candles. See CANDLEMAS.

Blessing of chalk. The Roman ritual included a blessing of the chalk used to mark the doors at the BLESSING OF HOUSES at Epiphany.

Blessing of Easter eggs. The decoration and blessing of eggs, derived from pre-Christian fertility celebrations, was incorporated into Christianity as a sign and celebration of the resurrection.

Blessing of the family. The blessing of a family by the father, marking each forehead with the sign of the cross, was long a widespread New Year custom.

Blessing of the font. Part of the Easter Vigil, included in the thanksgiving for baptism said over the baptismal water.

Blessing of food at Easter. The popular custom originated as a check on overindulgence after the Lenten fast.

Blessing of houses. A custom observed at the Epiphany, deriving from the Gospel for the feast telling of the Magi entering "the house" to worship the newborn King. The priest goes about the parish blessing houses and marking the lintels with the numerals of the current year and the initials of the traditional names of the Magi (Kaspar, Melchior, Balthasar), separated by crosses: +19+K+M+B+91+.

Blessing of lambs. An Easter custom recorded as early as the seventh century (BOBBIO MISSAL). Lamb was long a favorite food at Easter because of its association with the Passover (Exodus 12:8) and the sacrificed Lamb of God.

Blessing of nature. A blessing of the countryside, farms, orchards, fields, gardens, produce, the ocean, and fishing boats took place on August 15 since ancient times. The roots of such customs seem to be in pre-Christian fertility or harvest festivals.

Blessing of the new fire. The beginning of the Easter Vigil during which the new fire is struck as a remembrance of creation and of the resurrection.

Blessing of the waters. A custom observed in the Eastern churches on the feast of the Epiphany, based on the understanding that Christ, by his baptism in the Jordan River, consecrated all the waters of the earth. Among the Slavs, the blessing sometimes takes place in milder weather, the 25th day of Easter, mid-PENTECOST.

Blessing of wine. A custom in many churches in northern Europe and

England in the Middle Ages. Wine was blessed on St. John's Day (December 27), because of the legend that St. John had been given a cup of poisoned wine and was unharmed. The blessed wine was then given to brides and grooms at the conclusion of wedding celebrations during the ensuing year. The cup was known as the Love of St. John.

Boat (Old English). An oval container for incense carried by a server in procession for replenishing the THURIBLE or CENSER. See NAVICULA.

Bobbio missal (bo-BEE-o). An important collection of liturgical texts dating from the mid-eighth century; the missal is of Gallican provenance, with Irish influence, and has been named for the important monastery in the small town of Bobbio, Italy, in the Apennines some forty miles northeast of Genoa, in whose library it was collected with other early manuscripts.

Bobeche (boe-BESH; modern French). A collar, usually of glass, on a candle socket to catch drippings.

Bowing (Old English). Since early times Christians have bowed at the name of Jesus (Philippians 2:10); bowing to the altar and crucifix developed later. In the medieval period it became customary to bow at the name of the Holy Trinity in the GLORIA PATRI, at the description in the NICENE CREED of the Holy Trinity as "worshiped and glorified," and at the SANCTUS.

Bread. Originally in Christian celebrations of the Holy Communion leavened bread was used, being an element of standard fare; it remains the practice of the Eastern church and many Protestant denominations. Later, based on the understanding of the Eucharist as a Christian celebration of the Passover, the Last Supper being understood as a Passover meal, unleavened bread became customary in the Western church.

Breviarium Sanctae Crucis (brevi-ARE-ee-um SANKT-eye CREW-chis; Latin, Breviary of the Holy Cross). A reformed breviary prepared by order of the pope in 1535 by Francisco Cardinal de Quinones (d. 1540) and named after the cardinal's titular church. The breviary reduced the complexity of the ranking of feasts and simplified the office by the elimination of antiphons, versicles, and the Little Office of Our Lady; it provided for the praying of the whole psalter each week and the reading of nearly the entire Bible each year. It had an influence on Thomas Cranmer's revision of the office for the *Book of Common Prayer*. It was proscribed by Paul IV in 1558.

Breviary (Latin *breviarium*, abridgement, summary). A book which contains the daily prayer of the church.

Bright Week. The name in the Eastern churches for what in the West is called HOLY WEEK.

Broach (Middle English, a spike, pin). A spire which springs immediately from the top of a tower without any intermediary stage or parapet.

Brocade (bro-CADE; from Italian *broccato*, embossed fabric). A fabric woven with a raised design, often used for PARAMENTS and vestments. See DAMASK.

Brotsonntag (BROTE SOHN-tahg; German, bread Sunday). A German name, until the twentieth century, for Laetare, the fourth Sunday in Lent, deriving from the Gospel appointed for the Sunday, John 6:1-15.

Budded cross. See CROSS.

Burse (Latin *bursa*, bag, purse). A flat, stiff envelope covered with fabric in the color of the season, in which the CORPORAL and PURIFICATORS are carried to and from the altar.

Busstage (BOOSE-tahg-e; German, repentance days). Days of penance proclaimed by German rulers from time to time, especially in Advent and Lent.

Butterfly (Middle English). A symbol of resurrection. As a larva it represents human life; its life in the cocoon corresponds to the time in the tomb, waiting for the resurrection; in its final stage it emerges from the grave and soars to heaven with a new body.

Buttress (Middle English). A structure, usually brick or stone, built against a wall for support or reinforcement.

Byzantine rite. The use of the Eastern churches, both Orthodox and Uniate (those subject to the pope), deriving their liturgy from Byzantium (Constantinople). The eucharistic rite is in two forms: the LITURGY OF ST. BASIL and its abbreviated form, the LITURGY OF ST. JOHN CHRYSOSTOM.

Cc

Caeremoniarius (ser-i-moan-AH-ree-us). The Latin name of the master of ceremonies, necessary for the efficient conduct of a complicated religious service. It is the responsibility of this minister to supervise the entire liturgical action, directing and reminding the other ministers so their attention to what they are doing can be undistracted.

Cambridge Camden Society. An organization, later known as the Ecclesiological Society, that promoted the cause of the Gothic in church architecture and decoration. John Mason Neale (1818-1886) was a leading member.

Campanile (kamm-pan-EE-lay; Italian from Latin *campana*, a bell [made of metal produced in Campania]). A free-standing bell tower.

Candlemas. The feast of the Presentation of Our Lord in the Temple (and the Purification of St. Mary the Virgin), February 2. Because the Gospel for the day includes the song of Simeon, the NUNC DIMITTIS, which praised Christ as "a light to lighten the Gentiles," it became customary at mass on that day to bless CANDLES for use in church for the coming year, hence the name candle-mass. The Roman Sacramentary and the Episcopal *Book of Occasional Services* provide rites for such blessing of candles.

Candles (Old English from Latin *candere*, to shine). The use of candles in the church grew out of processional lights which, in early times, stood beside the altar. The lights were for utilitarian purposes with the exception of the lamp that was lighted at sundown and that burned throughout the night, the lighting of which involved ceremonies similar to those of the Service of Light (LUCERNARIUM) at the beginning of Evening Prayer in the *Lutheran Book of Worship* and the *Book of Common Prayer.* Because of the symbolism which came to associate candles with Christ the light of the world, ancient regulations required candles to be made of pure beeswax; this was later mitigated to requiring a minimum of 51 percent (i.e., more than half) beeswax. Unbleached candles of an orange color were used during PASSIONTIDE and in connection with the burial of the dead. The most common use was a single pair of candles on or near the altar, which are sometimes explained as representing the two natures of Christ the light of the world. A frequent practice was to have two candles on the altar, two on the RIDDEL posts, and two on the pavement. As riddels became less and less common, the additional candles were placed on the altar, and from this consolidation came the recent practice of placing six candles on the altar (the central crucifix being explained as the seventh candle; see Revelation 1:12-13). Branched candlesticks, in the Western church, are technically Vesper lights and were introduced into the West for Vespers of the Blessed Sacrament. See DIKIRION and TRIKIRION.

Canon (Latin, rule). 1. One of a chapter of priests serving a CATHEDRAL or collegiate church. 2. A church law or code of laws. 3. (From Latin *canon actionis*, the order of the action.) The GREAT THANKSGIVING, specifically the eucharistic prayer from the POST-SANCTUS through the GREAT AMEN. 4. A book containing the ORDINARY of the mass and prayers before and after, the use of which is a privilege of bishops in the Roman Catholic church.

Canonical hours. An older name for the daily prayer of the church, required of all the clergy: MATINS, LAUDS, PRIME, TERCE, SEXT, NONE, VESPERS, COMPLINE. Now called the LITURGY OF THE HOURS.

Canonization. Official recognition of a saint. The term derives from the practice of reading the names of saints during the CANON of the mass.

Canons of Hippolytus. A fourth-century Syrian adaptation of the *Apostolic Tradition*, once mistakenly thought to be the Roman Church order.

Cantate (kahn-TAH-tay). The name given to the fourth Sunday after Easter in medieval missals and in Lutheran use, from the first word of the INTROIT for the day: "O sing (*cantate*) unto the Lord a new song." In Lutheran churches, the name gave rise to the recognition on that Sunday of the work of choirs (even though nothing else in the propers suggested that emphasis).

Cantemus Domino (can-TAY-moose DOM-in-oh). Latin, "I will sing to the Lord," the song of Moses and Miriam from Exodus 15. It is appointed for use following the fourth lesson (Exodus 14:10-15:1) in the Easter Vigil (the third lesson in the Roman rite) and is also appropriate for use as the Old Testament canticle in Morning Prayer, especially during Easter. *Cantemus Domino*, in addition to appearing in the text of the Easter Vigil, is Canticle 19 in the *Lutheran Book of Worship*; Canticle 8 in Morning Prayer, Rite II in the *Book of Common Prayer*; and the canticle in Morning Prayer on Saturday of Week I in the Roman Liturgy of the Hours.

Canticle (KAN-ti-kal; Middle English from Latin *canticulum*, little song). A song, other than a psalm, usually taken from the Bible and used in the services of the church.

Cantillation (Latin *cantillare*, to sing in a low voice, to hum). Chanting, intoning, reciting in a musical monotone.

Cantionales (can-shun-ALS). Books of Lutheran service music containing intonations for the minister, the chant of the choir, and the hymns of the congregation, first prepared in the sixteenth century. The famous ones are by Johann Spangenberg (1545) and Lucas Lossius (1561).

Cantor (CAN-ter; Latin, singer; from *cantare*, to sing). A leader of singing, especially unaccompanied song.

Cantoris (Latin, of the cantor). The traditional place of the cantor, on the north (left) or Gospel side of the chancel; **decani** (Latin, of the dean), the place of the dean, in cathedral churches is on the south or epistle side (to the right as one faces the altar from the congregation).

Capitulum (ca-PIT-u-lum; Latin, little chapter). A verse or brief passage of Scripture read at certain offices of daily prayer, notably at COMPLINE.

Cappa magna (CAP-a MAG-na; Latin, large cape). A full cloak with a deep hood worn by doctors in English universities and by archbishops and bishops in the Roman Catholic church.

Cappa nigra (CAP-a NIG-ra; Latin, black cape). A hooded black cloak worn by clergy during CHOIR OFFICES, originating when churches were unheated, and in outdoor processions.

Caput jejunii (KAH-poot je-JUNE-ee-ee; Latin, head, beginning of the fast). The title of Ash Wednesday in the GELASIAN SACRAMENTARY.

Carillon (KAR-i-lon, kah-RILL-yon; French, from Latin *quaternio*, set of four [bells]). A range of a minimum of fifteen bells designed to play polyphonic music.

Carol (Old French from Greek *choraules*, a piper for a choral dance). A song, especially a joyful song, originally sung to accompany a circular dance. Now a traditional and popular song of a religious character, distinguished from a hymn by being a popular, unpolished composition for informal singing; hymns are written by educated authors for formal use in the services of the church.

Cassock (KASS-uk; Italian *cassaca*, the basic garment of ordinary people in the Middle Ages). An ankle-length black garment, close fitting to the waist with a fuller skirt, worn by clergy, choir, musicians, and servers; the basic garment of those who minister in the church, and over which the vestments were worn. It is an undergarment and not itself a vestment. Over the cassock is worn the SURPLICE or COTTA; in the past, the ALB was worn over the cassock.

Catechesis (cat-a-KEE-sis; from Greek *katekhein*, to teach by word of mouth). The instruction and training given to CATECHUMENS.

Catechumen (CAT-a-cue-men; Middle English from Greek *katekhein*, to teach orally by question and answer). A person preparing for Holy Baptism by undergoing instruction and training in the Christian life. In Lutheran use, the name was often applied to a person baptized in infancy who was receiving catechetical instruction leading to CONFIRMATION.

Catechumenate (cat-a-CUE-men-it). The period of instruction and training which catechumens undergo in preparing for Holy Baptism.

Cathedra (cath-EE-dra; Greek, chair). The bishop's chair in the CATHEDRAL church. Its original position, being recovered in modern times, was behind the main altar, in the center of the APSE. From this chair the bishop preached and gave formal instruction and teaching, for sitting was the position of authority in the ancient world. The bishop's chair was therefore a symbol of authority; it remains an important symbol of the office.

Cathedral (cath-EE-dral; Middle English from Greek *cathedra*, chair, throne). The church of a diocese in which the bishop's chair, the CATHEDRA, is located. It is not simply any large or ornate church.

Cathedral office. The form of Morning and Evening Prayer, consisting primarily of psalmody and intercession; the simple, daily public prayer of Christianity celebrated in cathedrals and in parish churches. The name derives from the *ordo cathederalis* (order of the cathedral) of the Mozarabic rite. In the **monastic office,** the services were more complex with hymns and antiphons, and Scripture readings, and especially the praying of the entire psalter within a brief period, such as one week or less.

Catholic (Greek *kata*, according to, and *holos*, the whole). Whole, complete. A person or church which receives the Christian faith entirely and intact without alteration or selection in matters of faith. The opposite of catholic is heretic (Greek *haireo*, I choose), one who selects which parts of the faith are acceptable. Catholic is thus more specific than "Christian" and is not a synonym for "ecumenical," "worldwide," or "universal."

Cautel (KAW-tell; Latin *cautela*, caution). A rubrical direction, especially those prefixed to the 1570 Roman missal, for the correct administration of the sacraments to give the minister guidance in case of accidental faults during the service.

Celebration (Latin *celebrare*, to frequent, fill, celebrate). The solemn performance of a religious rite, especially Holy Baptism and Holy Communion.

Celtic cross. See CROSS.

Celtic rite (KELL-tik; SELL-tik). The liturgy of the church in the British Isles before the mission of St. Augustine of Canterbury (596-597). The principal surviving liturgical books are the BANGOR ANTIPHONARY, the STOWE MISSAL, and the BOBBIO MISSAL.

Censer (SEN-ser; Old French *encens*, incense). A closed container in which incense is burned; also called a **thurible**. See Numbers 4:5-8; Leviticus 16:2, 12-13; Revelation 8:3-5.

Cento (SEN-toe; Latin, a patchwork). A literary work, especially a poem or a hymn translation, pieced together from the works of several authors.

Cere cloth (SEER; Middle English from Latin *cera*, wax). A cloth the exact size of the MENSA of the altar, treated with wax to resist moisture and to prevent the oils poured on the altar at its consecration from staining the linens. On stone altars, for which its use originated, it is the first cloth on top of the altar, lying beneath the FAIR LINEN. It is of course unnecessary when the problems it was designed to resist are not present.

Ceremonial (Middle English from Latin *caerimonia*, sacredness, religious rite). The prescribed actions or movements which are part of the performance of a rite or part of the liturgy.

Chaburah (HAB-ur-ah; Hebrew *chaber*, a friend). In Jewish practice, an informal band of friends who gathered for devotional purposes; they met weekly for supper. The activity has been proposed as a model for Christ and his disciples and their Last Supper.

Chaldean pattern of the anaphora. See EAST SYRIAN.

Chalice (CHAL-iss; Middle English from Latin *calix*, cup). The cup used in the celebration of the Holy Communion to contain the wine. A chalice was traditionally made of precious metal, gold or silver lined with gold, and has four parts: the bowl or cup, the stem, the knop or knob on the middle of the stem, and the foot or base, which is larger in diameter than the cup to prevent tipping over.

Chancel (CHAN-sel; Middle English from Latin *cancelli*, lattice work, screen). That portion of a church building beyond the NAVE and containing the CHOIR and the SANCTUARY; the space at the liturgically EAST end of the nave.

Chancel rail. See ALTAR RAIL.

Chant (Middle English from Latin *cantare*, to sing). A melody adopted for singing unmetrical verses.

Chantry (CHAN-tree; Middle English). A separate chapel, usually containing the tomb of the founder or builder of a church or monastery.

Chapel (Middle English from Latin *capella*, originally a shrine containing the cape [*cappa*] of St.

Martin of Tours). A subordinate enclosure or building sheltering an altar other than the principal altar of a church.

Chapel of ease. A chapel established by a large parish church where distance from the parish makes attendance difficult, the aim of which, often long delayed, is independent status.

Chapter (Middle English from Latin *caput*, head). 1. A short lesson read at certain of the hours of daily prayer; the CAPITULUM. 2. A body consisting of the DEAN and CANONS of a CATHEDRAL.

Chasuble (CHAS-you-bul; Latin *casula*, little house). The principal outer garment worn by the PRESIDING MINISTER when celebrating the Holy Communion, made usually of silk or BROCADE in the color of the liturgical season, often ornamented with ORPHREYS. It has its origin in a poncho-like garment worn in ancient Rome and is now a principal liturgical sign of ordination. The traditional prayer while vesting associates the chasuble with the yoke of Christ: "Lord, you have said, 'My yoke is easy and my burden is light.' Make me so to bear it that I may enjoy you forever." In the medieval style, the orphreys on the back of the chasuble suggested a yoke, being in the shape of a Y with the upper arms going to the shoulders of the priest. The Byzantine chasuble is called a PHELONION.

Chi rho (kye rowe). The first two letters of the Greek XPICTOC, Christ; hence a monogram for Christ.

Chimere (sha-MEER; Old French *chamarre*, a loose light gown). A sleeveless gown of silk or satin worn by Anglican bishops as part of their full dress on civic occasions (it is not properly a liturgical vestment) and by doctors of divinity as part of their academic dress. Wide lawn sleeves were sometimes attached to this gown.

Choir (Middle English from Latin *chorus*, a dance). 1. A body of singers who assist in rendering musically the services of the church. 2. That part of the church building between the NAVE and the SANCTUARY with places for the clergy and the singers. To differentiate it from the choir of singers, it is sometimes in English practice spelled Quire, as in older English.

Choir Offices (Latin *officium*, performance of a duty). The services of the daily prayer of the church, especially Morning and Evening Prayer, so called because they were sung in the choir of the building rather than at the altar.

Chorale (kor-AL; German *choral* [*gesang*], choral [song]). 1. A harmonized hymn, especially one for the organ. 2. A choir or chorus.

Chorister (CORE-iss-ter; Middle English). A choir singer, especially a choirboy.

Chorrock (German, choir gown, robe). The black gown of European clergy, also called a TALAR.

Chrism (Old English from Greek *khrisma*, ointment). A mixture of oil and a fragrance, used in the anointing in Holy Baptism.

Chrisom (variant of CHRISM). The white robe put on one at baptism, perhaps to prevent the CHRISM from being rubbed off.

Christen (Old English from *Christen*, Christian). To give a name to at baptism; to baptize, make a Christian.

Christian flag. A flag with a body of white and a blue field bearing a red Latin cross, designed for an American Methodist Sunday school picnic at the beginning of the twentieth century.

Christmas (Old English *Christes mass*). 1. The annual celebration on December 25 of the birth of Christ. 2. The twelve days from December 25 until the Epiphany, January 6.

Christus Rex (Latin, Christ the King). An ancient form of the CRUCIFIX, revived in recent practice, showing Christ clothed as priest and prophet and crowned as king, reigning from the tree of the cross.

Church order (Latin *ordo*, order, originally a row of threads in a loom). An official publication containing regulations and directions for the government and worship of the church; for example,

the *DIDACHE*. More specifically, one of the provincial Lutheran liturgical books mostly of the sixteenth century, promulgated by secular magistrates, which contained doctrinal discussions, forms of service, rules for the church, school, and institutions. The Lutheran church orders may be classified under three groups. The largest and most important, representing the orders of central and northern Germany, includes Luther's two orders (1523, 1526); the orders by Bugenhagen (Brunswick [1528], Hamburg [1529], Luebeck [1531], Pomerania [1535], Denmark [1537], Schleswig-Holstein [1542], and Hildesheim [1544]); Wittemberg (1533), Duke Henry of Saxony (1539), Mecklenburg (1540, 1552), Hannover (1536), Brandenburg-Nuremberg (1533); and the Swedish Mass of 1531 by Olavus Petri. The second group, the ultraconservative orders, includes Brandenburg (1540), Pfalz-Neuburg (1543), Austria (1571), and Riga (1530). The third group shows the influence of Calvinism and includes Wuerttemberg (1553, 1559), Bucer's orders for Strasbourg, Baden (1556), Worms (1560), Rhein-Pfalz (1557).

Church year. The calendar of the church's seasons, the church's way of marking the passing of time and using the progress of the seasons to celebrate the life of Christ, beginning with ADVENT and continuing through the celebration of the incarnation and epiphany of Christ, his baptism, passion, death, resurrection, ascension, sending of the Spirit, and return in glory. The year as it now exists developed over many centuries, but nonetheless has a harmonious and eloquent logic.

Church year, announcement of. See ANNOUNCEMENT OF THE CHURCH YEAR.

Churching of women (Old English *circe*, church). A service of thanksgiving after childbirth, performed for the mother, based on the Jewish rite of purification (Leviticus 12). The custom is mentioned in a letter by Augustine of Canterbury to Gregory the Great, but the oldest extant forms of the service are medieval.

Ciborium (sib-OR-ee-um; Greek *kiborion*, a cup). 1. A CHALICE-shaped vessel with a lid, used to hold the bread in the form of hosts or wafers for Holy Communion. 2. A wood, stone, or metal canopy over an altar; a BALDACHINO.

Cincture (SINK-tscher; Latin *cinctura*, a girdle, belt). A rope or band of fabric worn around the waist of an ALB or CASSOCK, unnecessary with modern flowing albs. The traditional prayer while vesting, developed by celibate male priests, associates the cincture symbolically with chastity: "Lord, gird me with the cincture of purity and extinguish in my loins the desire of lust so that the virtue of continence and chastity may remain with me always." See ZONI.

Circle. An ancient symbol for eternity and unity, being without beginning and without end. A triangle enclosed within the circle represents the Holy Trinity; three interwoven circles also symbolize the Trinity, three in one.

Circumcision (sir-come-SIZGH-un). A name of the feast celebrated January 1. Since the circumcision of Christ was not a new or Christian rite, the name has disappeared from twentieth-century calendars and the day is given to the celebration of the mother of God (Roman Catholic church) or the Holy Name of Jesus (Episcopal and Lutheran churches).

Clementine liturgy. A name given to the outline of a mass inserted into the description in the *APOSTOLIC CONSTITUTIONS* of the consecration of a bishop.

Clerestory (CLEAR-story; Middle English, lighted story [of a building]). The top horizontal division of the NAVE of a church having three or five aisles.

Clerical address (Greek *kleros*, lot, inheritance; an office allotted, then the one to whom the office was allotted). **Reverend** (Latin *reverendus*, revered) has been used as a title of respect for Christian clergy since the fifteenth century. In America, Protestants of all stripes regularly called their clergy **father** for nearly two centuries. (A literary example is Father Mapple, the minister of the Whaleman's Chapel, in

Melville's *Moby Dick.*) The title derives in large measure from the clergy's classical learning, for in ancient Rome a member of the senate was called a father. Halfway through the twentieth century, Lutheran clergy were still addressed in convention and open letters as "fathers and brethren." **Mister** was the address of Roman Catholic priests until the middle of the nineteenth century, when the influx of Irish priests who were regularly called "father" introduced a new custom. In the nineteenth century, church colleges proliferated and with them a large supply of honorary doctorates, so Protestant clergy (sometimes even without the doctorate) came to be addressed as **doctor** (Latin, teacher). "Reverend" used with the last name only, as for example "Reverend Swenson," is as inappropriate as calling civil servants "Honorable Schmidt." The correct form is "The Reverend" with the whole name: The Rev. Helmut F. X. Swenson, for "The Rev." is a title of respect, not a noun or modifier of the surname, as if only one Swenson were reverend. **Pastor** (Latin, shepherd) is a biblical, traditional (and in English genderfree) noun which serves well as an ecumenical title for clergy.

Clerical dress. For the first three centuries clergy wore no special or distinctive clothing when presiding at services of the church. The requirement was simply that the clothing be clean. About the beginning of the fourth century a distinction began to be made between everyday clothing and the vestments worn for divine service, especially the ORARION, or primitive stole. Special dress for the clergy outside the church building did not exist before the sixth century. The garb worn by clerics was a conservative version of everyday wear: the old Roman dress of a *collobium* or tunic without sleeves and a *dalmatica* or *tunica manicata et talaris*, a long white coat with sleeves. Black has been the color of the dress of clerics since the seventeenth century. In the United States, the Third Plenary Council of Baltimore (1884) required Roman Catholic clergy to wear the Roman collar and a coat of black or somber color outside the house; the Roman collar and cassock at home and in the church.

Cloister (CLOY-stir; Middle English from Latin *claustrum*, an enclosed place). An external covered passage ordinarily surrounding or forming a square.

Close (CLOZE; Middle English from Latin *claudere*, to close). The enclosed confines of the property of a CATHEDRAL or other building.

Closed time (*Tempora clausa*). A period during which marriages are not performed. Lent has been such a time since the Council of Laodicaea (363).

Coadjutor (koh-ad-JOO-ter; Middle English from Latin *adjutare*, to assist). An assistant bishop who has the right of automatic succession to the SEE.

Cock. 1. A symbol of watchfulness. 2. As a passion symbol it represents Peter, who denied Jesus before the cock crowed on the morning of the crucifixion (Matthew 26:74-75; Mark 14:72; Luke 22:60-61; John 18:27).

Collect (KOLL-ekt; Middle English from Latin *collecta*, assembly, and *collectus*, collected). A brief, carefully ordered prayer according to a strict pattern (address, reason, petition, result, termination), characterized by economy and compression of language, which gathers the prayers of the people after they have themselves gathered for worship.

Color sequence. A sequence of liturgical colors is first found in the twelfth century, but a standard sequence for the Western church did not become general until much later. There came to be five colors: violet was used for Advent and Lent; white was used during Christmas and Easter, on festivals of Christ, of the saints who were not MARTYRS, and on Trinity Sunday; red was used on the Day of Pentecost, on the feasts of martyrs, and during Holy Week; green was used during the time after the Epiphany and after Pentecost; black was used on Good Friday and for funerals. Rose pink was sometimes used on the third Sunday in Advent (*Gaudete*) and the fourth Sunday in Lent (*Laetare*); blue was sometimes used in Advent. In the Eastern church no definite rules prevail except for the general rule (followed anciently in the West also) of using the best vestments on the holiest days.

Comes (KOH-mays; Latin *liber comitis*, a handbook). A book listing, or later providing, the texts of the passages of the Bible to be read at mass, arranged according to the church year. Such books, giving the full texts of the PERICOPES, began to appear in the fifth century.

Comfortable Words. Four New Testament passages given in the *Book of Common Prayer* (Matthew 11:28; John 3:16; 1 Timothy 1:15; 1 John 2:1—the last three were from Archbishop Hermann's Consultation, the first was added by the Anglican Reformers), said by the celebrant after the ABSOLUTION to confirm it, for it was a principle of the Anglican Reformers and others that absolution is received through the promise of the word of God rather than merely by the words of the priest.

Commemoration. 1. The remembrance of a saintly person on a specific day, usually the date of the person's death and birth into heaven. 2. The recognition of a lesser festival, falling on the same day as a greater, by using the COLLECT (and SECRET and

POST-COMMUNION) of the lesser feast after the corresponding prayer of the greater.

Commination (KOM-in-ay-shun; Middle English from Latin *comminari*, to threaten). A penitential rite for Ash Wednesday in the *Book of Common Prayer*, giving God's denunciation of sinners (from Deuteronomy 27), an exhortation to repentance and an assurance of pardon, Psalm 51, Kyrie, Lord's Prayer, suffrages and collects, an anthem (Jeremiah 31:18; Joel 2:12-13, 17; Habakkuk 3:2; Psalm 51:1; and the first antiphon sung in the medieval office during the distribution of ashes). The office has been in the English Prayer Book since 1549 (the name dates from the 1552 book) and was based on the penitential service that preceded the blessing of ashes in the SARUM RITE. It was intended for use prior to the celebration of Holy Communion. A revised form of the rite appeared in the American Prayer Book from 1892 through 1928.

Commingling. Placing a piece of consecrated bread in the chalice containing the consecrated wine to indicate the unity of the body and blood of Christ and, when the bread comes from a previous mass, the unity of all celebrations of the Sacrament.

Common. PROPERS for the Eucharist and the daily office appointed for a class of persons who do not have an individual proper of their own; for example, the common of saints or the common of martyrs.

Commune (come-YOON; Middle English *communen*, to share). To receive Holy Communion.

Communicant. One who receives, or who is entitled to receive, Holy Communion.

Communicantes (komm-you-ni-CAHN-tays). The third part of the Roman CANON, a later addition attributed to Pope Gelasius, beginning *Communicantes* ("In fellowship with . . . " [various saints are named]).

Communicate (Latin *communicare*, to make known). To receive Holy Communion.

Communio (kom-YOU-nee-oh; Latin, communion), **communion verse**. A verse, usually from Scripture, forming an element of the PROPER, sung during or after the communion of the people.

Communio sanctorum (sank-TOR-um). A Latin phrase from the Apostles' Creed, perhaps deliberately ambiguous, that can mean either "communion of holy persons" (the **communion of saints**) or "communion in holy things."

Communion. 1. The communion verse, COMMUNIO. 2. The reception of the Holy Communion.

Competentes (kom-pa-TEN-tays; Latin *competere*, to seek or strive together). In the ancient church, those admitted to the final stage of preparation for baptism; also called *electi*, the elect, or in the

East, *photisomenoi*, the illuminated, enlightened.

Completuria (kom-pla-TURE-i-a; Latin, completion). The post-communion, a brief prayer of thanksgiving after communion.

Compline (KOMM-plin; Middle English from Latin *completorium*, completion). The last of the traditional hours of daily prayer, prayed at the end of the day before going to sleep.

Computus (komm-PEW-tuss; Latin, determination). The collection of rules by which the date of Easter is calculated. In earlier times, before calendars were easily available, a knowledge of the computus was an essential part of the training of the clergy.

Concelebration (Latin *com*, together, *celebrare*, to frequent, celebrate). The joint celebration of the Eucharist by two or more priests who join in saying the central parts of the CANON, especially the VERBA. The practice was probably usual in the early church, especially when presbyters joined their bishop in celebrating mass, but it gave way to individual celebrations of the Eucharist. The practice was restored to Roman use by the Second Vatican Council in 1963. It has continued in the Eastern churches to the present.

Concertato (kahn-sir-TAH-toe; Latin, joined together). 1. A style of musical composition that suggests combined and contrasting

use of vocal and instrumental forces, common in the Baroque era (1600-1750). 2. Recently, a type of composition, usually hymn-based, in which choral and instrumental forces are combined and contrasted with congregational song by stanzas.

Concomitance (con-KOMM-i-tance; Latin *comitari*, to accompany). The doctrine that the whole Christ is present and received under each KIND in Holy Communion. Thus those who receive only the consecrated bread or only the consecrated wine receive the whole Christ and not a deficient or partial communion.

Concurrence (Middle English from Latin *concurrere*, to run together). When two festivals fall on successive days so that second Vespers of the first overlaps first Vespers of the second festival. The propers of the more important day take PRECEDENCE and prevail. The collect of the more important festival is said first; the collect of the second is said next. See OCCURRENCE.

Confessio (con-FESS-ee-oh; Latin, confession, testimony). A crypt beneath the high altar and raised choir of a church, usually containing the burial place or relics of a saint.

Confession (Middle English from Latin *confessare*, to acknowledge). 1. The admission and acknowledgment of sin and guilt, which may liturgically be made in private before a confessor, or in public as part of a service of worship. 2. The profession of faith made by a MARTYR or CONFESSOR. 3. The tomb of a martyr.

Confessors. Those holy men and women who are commemorated on the church's calendar because of their fearless witness by their life and teaching to the truth of the Christian faith. The commemoration of the confessors began shortly after that of the MARTYRS.

Confirmand (KON-fir-mand; Latin *confirmandus*, gerundive of *confirmare*, to strengthen). A candidate for confirmation.

Confirmation (Middle English from Latin *confirmare*, to strengthen, make firm). An action, originally part of baptismal initiation, that became separated by several years from the baptism and was variously understood and interpreted as a giving of the Holy Spirit, a strengthening of one who had been baptized for the struggle of maturer life, a confirmation by the bishop of the baptismal action or the candidate's profession of faith, the assumption for oneself of the promises made on one's behalf at baptism. Confirmation began to be listed as a sacrament in the twelfth century.

Confitebor tibi (con-fi-TAY-bore tibby; Latin, [O Lord,] I will praise thee). A song of Isaiah (Isaiah 12:1-6), given in the Lutheran *Common Service Book* and the *Service Book and Hymnal* as Canticle 6; used in the Liturgy of the Hours as the canticle at Morning Prayer on Thursday in Week I. See *ECCE DEUS*.

Confiteor (con-FIT-ee-or; Latin, I confess). The confessional portion in preparation for mass, conducted anciently in the sacristy and later at the foot of the altar at the beginning of mass.

Confractoria (con-frak-TOR-ee-a; Latin *fractio*, breaking). Anthems sung during the FRACTION.

Consecration (Middle English from Latin *consecrare*, to make sacred). The act of setting apart something or someone for sacred use and service. In the Eucharist the consecration is the setting apart of the bread and wine for use in Holy Communion by praying the GREAT THANKSGIVING.

Consecration of a church. See DEDICATION OF A CHURCH.

Consubstantiation (Latin *com*, together). A name sometimes applied, but never by Lutherans themselves and indeed rejected by them, to the Lutheran doctrine of Christ's presence in the Sacrament of the Altar "in, with, and under" the forms of bread and wine, maintaining the coexistence of the substances of bread and wine and the body and blood of Christ.

Consuetudinary (con-swi-TOO-din-ary; Middle English from Latin *comsuescere*, to become accustomed to). The book containing rites and ceremonies for services or the rules and customs of discipline for a monastery, a religious order, or a cathedral. As the uniformity of the Roman rite spread, the need for such a local book declined.

Contakion or **Kontakion** (con-TAK-ee-on; Greek from *kontos*, a shaft [on which a vellum scroll would be wound]). In the Eastern churches a hymn in a series of strophes, expanding on the thought of the TROPARION.

Contestatio (kon-tess-TAT-see-oh; Latin, a supplication, earnest request). The usual name in Gallican and Spanish missals for the PREFACE of the Eucharist; also called ILLATIO or IMMOLATIO.

Conventicle (Middle English from Latin *conventiculum*, a place of meeting). A religious meeting, especially a secret or an illegal one, such as those held by dissenters in England and Scotland in the sixteenth and seventeenth centuries.

Cope (Old English from Latin *cap(p)a*, a cloak). A liturgical cape or cloak, usually in the color of the liturgical season, joined at the breast by a MORSE, and worn over the ALB or SURPLICE for processions and festival services other than the Eucharist. The use of the cope is not limited to ordained ministers.

Coptic rite. A rite of the church deriving from Alexandria, one of the three great patriarchates of the early church which, according to tradition, was founded by St. Mark. The normal liturgy is the LITURGY OF ST. BASIL. The Coptic church became MONOPHYSITE and increasingly isolated from the rest of Christianity.

Corbel (cor-BELL; Middle English from Latin *corvus*, a raven [corbels were originally wedge-shaped, suggesting the beak of a raven]). A projection from a wall, providing support for the beams which hold up the roof; often decorated with carvings or shields or symbols.

Corona (cor-OH-na; Latin, a crown). A large decorative crown suspended from the ceiling of a church, made to hold a large number of tapers.

Corporal (CORE-por-al; Latin *corporale*, pertaining to the body). A square of fine linen laid on the FAIR LINEN upon which the sacred vessels are placed from the OFFERING through the COMMUNION in the service of Holy Communion. Its dimensions are never greater than the depth of the MENSA from the front edge to the back. The cloth must always be scrupulously clean.

Corpus (KOR-puss; Latin, the body). The figure of Christ shown on a crucifix.

Corpus Christi (Latin, the body of Christ). The celebration, traditionally on the Thursday following Trinity Sunday, of the institution of the Sacrament of the Altar, the Holy Communion, characterized by masses and processions with the Blessed Sacrament. The celebration was instituted in 1264 because the somberness of LENT and the TRIDUUM made a festive celebration on Maundy Thursday undesirable. The Thursdays of Easter were part of the celebration of the resurrection, and the Thursday following WHITSUNDAY was, in the Middle Ages, part of the eight-day celebration of Pentecost. The Thursday after Trinity Sunday was therefore the first Thursday after Maundy Thursday open for the celebration. In the 1969 Roman calendar, the feast is called the Body and Blood of Christ.

Cotta (COT-a; Latin, a coat). A short, white, finger-tip length garment with elbow-length, wide sleeves, worn over a CASSOCK by servers, choristers, and organists.

Counterpoint. A system of musical composition in which four, eight, or twelve independent melodies are related to each other in a way that is agreeable; *puncta contra punctum* (point against point); the predecessor of much modern church music.

Cramp rings. Finger rings supposed to cure cramps, blessed in England by the king in his chapel on Good Friday because of "the special gift of curation ministered unto the kings of this realm."

Crèche (KRESH; Old French, a crib). A feeding trough for cattle and the crib of the infant Jesus, used in representations of the Nativity. The use of such a crèche was introduced by St. Francis of Assisi.

Credence (KREE-dinse; Middle English from Latin *credentia*, belief, trust). A side table or shelf on which the SACRAMENTAL VESSELS and the MISSAL STAND are kept until they are brought to the altar for the Holy Communion. The credence is appropriately covered with a white linen cloth. The name derives from a table holding food for testing to detect poison.

Crosier. Variant of CROZIER.

Cross (Old English from Latin *crux*, cross). The sign of Christ showing his principal work of salvation; thus the central sign of the Christian faith and the central ornament of an altar in the EASTWARD POSITION. Many forms of the cross have developed in Christian use: **anchor**, in which the top part of the anchor is in the shape of a cross, showing hope (Hebrews 6:19); **archepiscopal**, a PATRIARCHAL cross; **budded** or **botonee**, a Latin or Greek cross with trefoil ends, each suggesting the Holy Trinity; **Celtic**, similar to the Latin cross but with a circle surrounding the intersection of the arms; **Egyptian**, an ancient symbol of life, a cross with a loop at the top like a handle, suggesting the cross as the tree of life; **graded**, a Latin cross with three steps at the base, representing faith, hope, and charity (1 Corinthians 13:13); **Greek**, four arms of equal length;

Jerusalem or **crusaders' cross** consisting of four tau crosses meeting at the center, forming a Greek cross with a short cross bar at the end of each arm, and often shown with four Greek crosses in the four angles of the larger cross; **Latin**, with the upper arm and the two side arms of equal length and the lower arm twice as long as the part above the crossarm; **Lorraine**, chiefly heraldic, a Latin cross with an additional and longer arm near the base; **Maltese**, formed by touching the points of four spearheads together with the outer eight points equidistant from each other, said to represent the eight Beatitudes (Matthew 5:3-10); **(Eastern) Orthodox**, a Latin cross with a small cross arm near the top, representing the title Pilate put on the cross and a slanted arm where Jesus' feet were nailed; **papal**, three horizontal arms descending in increasing length; **patriarchal**, two horizontal arms near the top with the upper arm shorter than the lower crossarm; **St. Andrew** or **saltire**, having an X shape; **tau**, like a capital letter T; **Trinity** or **fleury**, a cross with equal arms and a fleur-de-lis at each end.

Crossing. The rectangular area in a cruciform church formed by the intersection of the NAVE and the TRANSEPTS.

Crown (Middle English from Latin *corona*, a garland, wreath). 1. The symbol of sovereignty, representing Christ as Lord and King of the universe. 2. The crown of thorns is a PASSION SYMBOL, recalling the suffering of Christ. 3.The reward of the faithful (1 Peter 5:4; Revelation 2:10). The crown is often shown with the cross, showing both aspects of the Christian life: cost and glory, suffering and triumph, death and resurrection.

Crozier or **crosier** (CROW-zee-er; Middle English from Old French *crossier*, a staff-bearer, from *crosse*, a bishop's staff). The pastoral staff carried by a bishop as a sign of office. It derives from a hook-top scepter, BACULUM, an ancient symbol of authority. In the Eastern church this developed into the T-shaped bishop's scepter; in the West it developed into the single-hooked shape that came to be regarded as a form of the shepherd's crook. The name originally signified the bearer of the bishop's cross, thus its derivation.

Crucifer (CREW-si-fer; Latin *crux*, a cross, and *ferre*, to carry). One who carries the processional cross.

Crucifix (Middle English from Latin *cruci fixus*, fastened to a cross). A cross bearing the image of the crucified Savior. In early times the figure of Christ was clothed as a priest and a prophet, crowned as a king (CHRISTUS REX), and shown alive in an attitude of blessing and triumph, with arms outstretched to either side in benediction and embrace, "reigning from a tree." By the tenth century the figure of Christ was commonly depicted in the agony of death, showing the cost of salvation. The representation passed into common Lutheran use throughout Europe and in many places in North America until North American Lutherans, to be like their Protestant neighbors, abandoned its use in favor of the plain cross. The crucifix may be said to be the preferred ornament of an altar in the EASTWARD POSITION.

Cruciform (CREW-si-form). Cross-shaped; ecclesiastical buildings with TRANSEPTS.

Cruet (CREW-ett; Norman-French, a little flask). A small pitcher made of glass to contain the wine for the Holy Communion or the water for cleansing the chalice.

Crusaders' cross. See CROSS, JERUSALEM.

Crypt (KRIPT; Greek *kryptos*, hidden). A vault beneath the church used as a chapel or burying place.

Cuffs. Decorated gauntlets called **epimankia** in the Greek church, worn at the wrist by deacons and priests in the Byzantine rite for convenience, and understood to signify trust in God and the bonds which bound the hands of Christ.

Cult (Latin *cultus*, cultivation, worship). The form and practice of the worship of a body of people; liturgical faith and practice.

Curate (CURE-et; Middle English from Latin *cura*, care). 1. One who has the care or "cure" of souls. 2. A cleric who serves as an assistant in a parish under the direction of the pastor or rector, usually with a limited term.

Cursus (CURSE-iss; Latin, course, march). A system of Latin accentual prose rhythm employed in late antiquity and in the later Middle Ages, produced by arranging the accents in the last syllables of a clause according to certain fixed rules. Three forms developed: *cursus planus* (plain course), as in the English phrase "honor forever"; *cursus tardus* (slow course), as in "fullness of joy in heaven"; and *cursus velox* (swift course), as in "mighty deliverance." This system of rhythm was used in the composition of the Latin collects and other prayers.

Dalmatic (dal-MAT-ik; Middle English from Latin *Dalmatica*, Dalmatian [garment]). A long, wide-sleeved garment originating in the ordinary dress of Dalmatia, hence its name; a vestment worn over the alb and stole by a DEACON (assisting minister) at the celebration of the Holy Communion. It is distinguished from the TUNICLE of the SUBDEACON by having two crossbars rather than one on the back (and front). It was introduced into the West by the Emperor Commodus at the end of the second century, and in the next century it became an imperial robe and, centuries later, a garb worn only by imperial favor. Probably for this reason the bishop of Rome vested his deacons in dalmatics. English monarchs are vested with a form of the dalmatic in the course of the coronation ceremonies. See STIKARION.

Damask (DAM-esk; Middle English from Latin [*pannus de*] *damasco*, cloth of Damascus). A firm, lustrous, reversable fabric of cotton, linen, silk, or wool, made with flat patterns in a satin weave on a plain-woven ground. A BROCADE is not reversable and has a slightly raised pattern.

Deacon (DEE-ken; Middle English from Greek *diakonos*, servant). 1. One of the three traditional forms of ordained Christian ministry, with the bishop and presbyter, the principal responsibility of whom is to represent Christ the servant by exercising a serving ministry to those in need, working with the workers of the world, and relating the church to the world. 2. In the liturgy, the principal ASSISTING MINISTER.

Deaconess (Middle English from Greek *diakonissa,* a fourth-century feminization of *diakonos*, deacon). A woman deacon (see Romans 16:1), charged in the early church with certain functions which were deemed inadvisable or improper for male deacons—ministering to sick and poor women, instructing women catechumens, assisting in the baptism of women. The office developed greatly in the third and fourth centuries and is described in the *APOSTOLIC CONSTITUTIONS*. In the nineteenth century the office was revived by the Moravians, brought into Lutheran use by Theodor Fliedner in Kaiserswerth, Germany, and introduced into the United States in 1849 by William Passavant. It spread to England, where the first Church of England deaconess was dedicated in 1861; the office was introduced among the Methodists in 1888 and was established in the Church of Scotland in the same year.

Dean (Middle English from Latin *decanus*, [one] set over ten). The head of a community or group: the dean of a cathedral is the first of the CANONS. In North American Lutheran use, a pastor who chairs an association of neighboring congregations.

Decani. See under CANTORIS.

Decollation (from Latin *decollare*, to behead). A Latinate name for the commemoration of the Beheading of St. John the Baptist (August 29).

Dedication of a church. Originally accomplished simply by the celebration of the Eucharist in the building. The earliest dedication of a Christian church is that of the Cathedral at Tyre in 314, described by Eusebius. During the fourth to the sixth centuries, as relics were incorporated into altars, a more elaborate **consecration** developed, presided over by a bishop, reaching a stable form in the thirteenth century that continued until modern times. Structures that were not designed to be permanent, such as wooden churches, and those that did not contain relics, were not consecrated but simply blessed, often by the priest. In Anglican practice the anniversary of the dedication of a church is observed annually on the first Sunday in October if the actual date of dedication is not known. The annual remembrance and celebration of the dedication of a church is a most desirable and salutary practice.

Departure of Mary. See ASSUMPTION.

Depositio (de-pos-IT-see-o; Latin, burial). A calendar designation that came to replace the earlier NATALE, the birthday of a martyr, as the focus shifted to the burial place and relics of departed saints.

Deprecation (dep-re-KAY-shun; Latin *deprecare*, to avert by entreaty). Prayer that evil may be removed or turned away; a portion of the Litany, "From all sin, from all error, from all evil...."

Descant (DESS-cant; Middle English from Latin *discantus*, a refrain). A melody which is complementary to the principal melody.

Descensus (de-SEN-sis; Latin, descended). The phrase in the APOSTLES' CREED referring to Christ's descent to the dead ("into hell" was the earlier English translation) between his death and his resurrection. The proper understanding of the problematic clause is disputed, and in the *Lutheran Book of Worship* the older translation of the Latin *descensus ad infernum* was retained because some Lutherans considered the translation "descended into hell" to be required by the Lutheran Confessions.

Desk (Middle English from Latin *desca*, a table). Any support or stand for a book used in the course of the service.

Deutsche Messe (German Mass). Luther's vernacular revision of the Eucharist, called The German Mass and Order of Service, 1526, more of a treatise than a liturgical form, intended as a service for the uneducated laity (those who did not know the classical languages). Choir parts of the Latin mass are made congregational hymns.

Diakonikon (dee-a-KON-i-kon; Greek, the deacon's book). A book containing the deacon's parts of the mass.

Didache (Greek, teaching [of the twelve apostles]). A first-century Syrian document of unknown authorship, the earliest example of a CHURCH ORDER, discovered in 1875 and first published in 1883.

Didascalia (did-as-CAL-ee-a; Greek, teaching). The Catholic Teaching of the Twelve Apostles and Holy Disciples of Our Savior. A CHURCH ORDER from the first half of the third century in northern Syria, modeled on the *DIDACHE* and embodied in the *APOSTOLIC CONSTITUTIONS*, formulating in an unmethodical arrangement teaching and rules for the Christian community, apparently by a physician who converted from Judaism, giving an instructive picture of how deeply the Gospel had permeated the lives of the clergy and people.

Dies irae, dies illa (DEE-ace EE-rye, DEE-ace ILL-la; Latin, day of wrath, that day). A famous thirteenth-century SEQUENCE, probably by Thomas of Celano, a Franciscan monk. Originally an Advent hymn, it became the sequence for the REQUIEM mass, and the intense and powerful hymn was translated into many languages and entered into most hymnals.

Dignus es (Latin, you are worthy). A song to the Lamb of God (Revelation 4:11; 5:9-10, 13), Canticle 18 in Morning Prayer, Rite II in the *Book of Common Prayer*; in the Liturgy of the Hours it is the New Testament canticle in Evening Prayer on Tuesday of Week I, II, III, and IV, and at other times.

Dignus est Agnus (Latin, worthy is the Lamb). A song to the Lamb of God given as Canticle 12 in the *Common Service Book* (Revelation 5:12-13; 15:3-4; 19:6) and a principal inspiration for the Lutheran HYMN OF PRAISE, "WORTHY IS CHRIST." The central section, *Magna et mirabilia* (Revelation 15:3-4), is in the Liturgy of the Hours the canticle at Evening Prayer on Friday of Weeks I, II, III, and IV, and in the *Book of Common Prayer* is Canticle 19, The Song of the Redeemed, in Morning Prayer, Rite

II. An adaptation of Revelation 19:1-7 is the canticle in the Liturgy of the Hours at Sunday Evening Prayer II of Weeks I, II, III, and IV.

Dikirion (di-KEE-re-on; Greek, two candles). A two-branched candlestick held by Byzantine bishops in their left hand while blessing the people. See TRIKIRION.

Diptych (DIP-tik; Greek, twofold). 1. In the early church, two clay or wax tablets in a bookcover type of case on which were written the names of those faithful departed who were to be remembered in the intercessions. This diptych is the parent of the triptych (three-leaved) and polyptych (multileaved) forms of the REREDOS. 2. Any list of names for intercession or commemoration.

Diskos (Greek, a dish). A Byzantine PATEN.

Divine Office (Middle English from Latin *officium*, the performance of a responsibility). The daily prayer of the church, consisting of the principal hours of Morning and Evening Prayer together with COMPLINE and the LITTLE HOURS. See OFFICE.

Divine Praises. A series of brief expressions of praise of God, Christ, and the saints, said as a reparation for blasphemous language and profanity and recited at the conclusion of BENEDICTION of the Blessed Sacrament before the HOST is replaced in the TABERNACLE: "Blessed be God. Blessed be his holy name. Blessed be Jesus Christ, true God and true man. Blessed be the name of Jesus. Blessed be Jesus in the most holy sacrament of the altar. Blessed be the great mother of God, Mary most holy. Blessed be the name of Mary, Virgin and Mother. Blessed be God in his angels and in his saints." The Divine Praises are thought to have been composed by Louis Felici ca. 1779. They have been supplemented by the addition of praise of the Immaculate Conception (1856), the Sacred Heart (1897), St. Joseph (1921), the Assumption (1950), the Precious Blood (1960), and the Holy Spirit (1964).

Doctors (Middle English from Latin *doctor*, a teacher). Those holy men and women who are remembered on the ecclesiastical calendar as teachers of the church.

Domine audivi (DOM-in-ay ow-DEE-wee). "O Lord, I have heard [thy speech]," a song from Habakkuk 3 given as Canticle 9 in the Lutheran *Common Service Book* and the *Service Book and Hymnal,* and in the Liturgy of the Hours at Morning Prayer on Friday of Week II.

Domine clamavi (clamm-AH-wee). "O Lord, I call to you," verses from Psalm 141 used as the psalm of repentance at Evening Prayer since ancient times. In the *Lutheran Book of Worship* the psalm begins with the antiphon "Let my prayer rise before you as incense" and appears in the text of Evening Prayer and as Canticle 5.

Dominica in albis (do-MIN-i-ca in AHL-biss; Latin, Sunday in white robes). A name in medieval missals for the Sunday after Easter, referring to the white robes worn by those baptized at Easter.

Dona (Latin, gifts). A Latin designation of the alms offered at a religious service.

Dormition. See ASSUMPTION.

Dorsal. Variant of DOSSAL.

Dossal (DOSS-el; Middle English from Latin *dorsum*, the back). A cloth hanging attached to the wall behind the altar. It may be in a liturgical color, but is usually of a neutral color.

Dove. The use of a dove (either live and set free to fly away, or a carved representation let down by a rope from the church ceiling) on Pentecost to signify the Holy Spirit was widespread in the Middle Ages. In the ornamentation of a church building, a descending dove represents the Holy Spirit, the life-giving energy essential in the celebration of Holy Baptism and Holy Communion.

Doxology (Greek *doxologia*, words of praise, glory). An ascription of praise to God. The GLORIA IN EXCELSIS is called the greater doxology; the GLORIA PATRI the lesser doxology. The conclusion of the Lord's Prayer is called its doxology. The concluding stanza of an OFFICE HYMN is traditionally a doxology to the Holy Trinity.

Dry mass (*missa sicca*). An abbreviated form of mass, lacking offertory, consecration, and communion, which developed in the Middle Ages, especially in France as a way of avoiding BINATION. A derisive name for the ANTE-COMMUNION.

Dust cloth. The topmost cover of an altar, used as a protector when the altar is not in use. It is often of a color other than white for practical reasons and as a reminder that it is to be removed before the altar is used in divine service.

Eagle. 1. In the Byzantine rite, a small circular rug with a representation of an eagle soaring over a city, on which a bishop stands during divine service, signifying the bishop's rule over his city as well as his purity and heavenly aspiration. 2. The symbol of St. John the Evangelist, derived from Ezekiel 1:10.

East. Liturgically the altar end of a church building, suggesting the rising sun and Jerusalem. ORIENTATING the church in this way is a confession of Christianity's eschatological confidence and expectation. A century and more ago, many congregations and architects went to ingenious lengths to maintain the proper eastward orientation of the church building on difficult sites.

East Syrian or **Chaldean**. A variation of the West Syrian pattern of the ANAPHORA, placing the EPIKLESIS after the INTERCESSIONS.

Easter (Old English, east). 1. The annual fifty-day celebration of the resurrection of Christ, beginning with the Easter Vigil and culminating on the Day of Pentecost. 2. Easter Day.

Easter Garden. A garden of flowers and plants around a represen-tation of a tomb, set up in a church at Easter to make vivid the phrase from the Gospel, "Now there was a garden in the place where he was crucified, and in the garden there was a new tomb in which no one had ever been laid" (John 19:41). The origins are doubtless pre-Christian, rooted in celebrations of the renewed fertility of the earth.

Easter Week. The seven days beginning with Easter Day and continuing until the second Sunday of Easter; the Easter OCTAVE. Easter Week is not a synonym for HOLY WEEK.

Eastern liturgies. The liturgies of the Eastern churches may be grouped in four families: **Antioch**, which influenced and eventually dominated that at Jerusalem, in two forms, the West Syrian (the Liturgy of St. James) and the East Syrian (Nestorian or Chaldean); **Alexandria** (the Liturgy of St. Mark) or the Egyptian rite, including the Coptic rite and the Ethiopic rite; **Constantinople** or the **Byzantine** rite (the Liturgy of St. John Chrysostom and the Liturgy of St. Basil), the dominant form, used by the Greeks, Russians, Melkites, and Ukrainians; **Armenia**.

Eastward position. An altar "in the eastward position" is an altar near or even against the liturgical EAST wall of a church.

Ecce Deus (EH-chay DAY-us; Latin, Behold, God [is my salvation]). The first song of Isaiah (Isaiah 12:2-6), given as Canticle 9 in Morning Prayer, Rite II in the *Book of Common Prayer*. See CONFITEBOR TIBI.

Ecclesiological Society. A later name of what was originally the CAMBRIDGE CAMDEN SOCIETY.

Ectene. See EKTENE.

Effeta or **Ephphetha** (EFF-fay-ta, EFF-fay-thah; Aramaic, be opened). The ritual opening of the ears and mouth of a candidate for baptism in the Roman rite, recalling Mark 7:34. The practice appears at an early date in the baptismal services for Holy Saturday at Rome and Milan.

Ego dixi (Latin, I said). The song of Hezekiah (Isaiah 38:10-20), given as Canticle 11 in the *Service Book and Hymnal* and in the Liturgy of the Hours as the canticle at Morning Prayer on Tuesday of Week II and at Morning Prayer in the Office of the Dead.

Egyptian. A variation of the West Syrian pattern of the ANAPHORA, placing the INTERCESSIONS after the PREFACE, which includes an offering.

Egyptian cross. See CROSS.

Eighteen benedictions. The principal prayer of supplication in the Jewish liturgy, called the *Tefillah* (prayer), recited while standing (thus called *'Amidah*), consisting of eighteen paragraphs each concluding with a benediction or blessing of one of the attributes of God (*'hatimah*, conclusion); the fourteenth of the benedictions has been divided into two so that now there are in fact nineteen of the blessings or benedictions.

Eileton (EYE-lay-tin; Greek, something wrapped around). In the Eastern church, a silk cloth spread on the altar during the liturgy, used beneath the ANTIMINSION; a counterpart to the Western CORPORAL.

Ekphonesis (ek-fone-EE-sis; Greek, an exclamation). A doxological conclusion of a prayer. The name derives from its being prayed aloud.

Ektene (ek-TAY-nay; Greek, earnest prayer). In the Byzantine liturgy, a litany consisting of petitions sung by the deacon to which the choir or congregation responds a number of times after the last petition, *Kyrie eleison* (Lord, have mercy); associated in Constantinople originally with outdoor processions. The Kyrie in the Holy Communion in the *Lutheran Book of Worship* is an adaptation of such a form.

Elements (Middle English from Latin *elementum*, rudiment). The bread and wine of the Holy Communion.

Elevation (Middle English from Latin *elevare*, to lift). Lifting up the bread and cup during the GREAT THANKSGIVING. An elevation is made at the words of institution relating to the bread and to the cup; at the conclusion of the Great Thanksgiving, both the bread and the cup are lifted together as a gesture of praise. Luther retained the elevation in his masses, and many of the important Reformation CHURCH ORDERS retained the gesture.

Ember Days (Old English *ymbrendagas*, recurring days). Four groups of three penitential days each, the Wednesday, Friday, and Saturday approximately at the turning of the seasons of the solar year: after St. Lucy's Day (December 13), after the first Sunday in Lent, after Pentecost, and after Holy Cross Day (September 14). Their origin and original purpose are obscure, but are probably connected with seedtime and harvest and vintage, the winter days being added later.

Embolism (EM-boll-ism; Middle English from Greek *embolismos*, thrown in). The liturgical expansion of the final petition of the Lord's Prayer. In the present Roman rite, after the congregation has prayed "Our Father . . . deliver us from evil," the celebrant prays, "Deliver us, Lord, from every evil, and grant us peace in our day. In your mercy keep us free from sin and protect us from all anxiety as we wait in joyful hope for the coming of our Savior, Jesus Christ." The congregation responds with the doxology "For the kingdom, the power, and the glory are yours, now and forever."

Enarxis (en-ARKS-iss; Greek, beginning). That portion of the Byzantine liturgy between the preparation at the PROTHESIS and the LITTLE ENTRANCE, consisting of three diaconal litanies, each followed by an antiphon.

Enrollment of candidates for baptism. The stage in the ancient progressive entrance into the Christian community, marking the conclusion of the catechumenate and the beginning of a still more profound preparation for the sacraments of initiation, involving the declaration of a commitment to a new way of living in preparation for baptism, a period of purification and illumination during which the scrutinies were performed and the creed and the Lord's Prayer were delivered and taught to the candidates.

Entrance rite. The opening action of the Eucharist during which the ministers enter the church and take their places. The entrance rite in its fullest, festive form consists of the entrance hymn or psalm, apostolic greeting, Kyrie, Hymn of Praise, and the collect of the day.

Epact (EE-pact; Old French from Greek *epaktai*, [days] brought in). 1. The number of days in the solar year above that in the lunar year of twelve months. 2. The number of days in the age of the moon on the first of January of a given year, used in determining the date of Easter.

Ephphetha. See EFFETA.

Epigonation (ep-ee-gone-AT-see-on; Greek, at the knee). An oblong piece of brocade suspended from the left hip of a priest of the Byzantine churches, signifying the sword of the Spirit and the towel with which Christ girded himself to wash the disciples' feet; conferred as a sign of honor. See PALITZA.

Epiklesis or **Epiclesis** (epp-i-CLAY-sis or e-PIK-le-sis; Greek, invocation). A prayer for the Holy Spirit as a part of the GREAT THANKSGIVING in the Eucharist or the thanksgiving over the water in Holy Baptism.

Epimankia. See CUFFS.

Epiphany (Middle English from Greek *epiphainein*, to appear). The annual celebration on January 6 of the manifestation of the divinity of Christ to the gentiles represented by the MAGI. Anciently and in the Eastern church still, the celebration centered primarily on the baptism of Christ and his first miracle at Cana in Galilee.

Epistle (ee-PISS-el; Middle English from Greek *epistole*, a letter). The biblical lesson immediately preceding the Holy Gospel in the Eucharist, drawn from a New Testament epistle, or the Acts, or Revelation. It is now often called simply the second lesson.

Epistle side. The liturgically south side of the sanctuary, that is the right side as one faces the altar, from which the epistle was read in the Middle Ages. See GOSPEL SIDE.

Epistler (ee-PISS-ler) or **Epistoler**. The person who reads or chants the EPISTLE in the Eucharist.

Epistolary. A book containing the EPISTLES read at mass.

Epitrakelion (ep-ee-tra-KELL-ee-on; Greek, on the neck). The wide priest's stole of the BYZANTINE RITE, joined in front for its entire length.

Eucharist (YOU-ker-ist; Middle English from Greek *eukharistia*, gratitude, thanksgiving). The service of the Holy Communion, the mass. The word is used with the definite article, the Eucharist; because the Eucharist is a service of thanksgiving, the form "Eucharist service" is redundant and is not used by those who know better.

Esto mihi (ESS-toe ME-he; Latin, be to me [a strong rock]). A name for Quinquagesima, the Sunday before Ash Wednesday in medieval calendars, from the first words of the Latin INTROIT.

Eucharistic lights. See LIGHTS.

Eucharistic prayer. The GREAT THANKSGIVING or sometimes, more specifically, the prayer of thanksgiving in the Holy Communion, the CANON.

Eucharistic vestments. In the Western church, traditionally the AMICE, ALB, CINCTURE, STOLE, MANIPLE, and CHASUBLE. In modern use, the maniple is seldom worn and the amice is often unnecessary if the alb has a collar. In the Eastern churches of the BYZANTINE RITE, the cassock, wide stole (EPITRAKELION), cincture (ZONI), cuffs (EPIMANIKIA), chasuble (PHELONION).

Euchologion (you-ko-LOW-gee-on; Greek, book of thanksgivings). A book containing the complete texts of the sacraments and blessings for various occasions.

Eulogy (YOU-la-gee; Middle English from Greek *eulogia*, praise). 1. Another name for the ANTIDORON. 2. An oration or statement extolling one recently deceased. Such praise is usually out of place in a funeral sermon, the purpose of which is to proclaim the Gospel of resurrection in Christ.

Evangeliary, Evangelistary (ev-an-GEL-e-ary, ev-an-gel-ISS-tary; Greek *evangelion*, announcement, good news). A book containing the PERICOPES from the four Gospels for reading at the Eucharist.

Evangelists' Days. The days on the ecclesiastical calendar commemorating the four evangelists,

two of whom are also apostles: Matthew (September 21), Mark (April 25), Luke (October 18), and John (December 27).

Evangelists' symbols. Based on Ezekiel 1:10 and 10:14, the traditional symbols are these: **Matthew**, a winged man or angel; **Mark**, a winged lion; **Luke**, a winged ox; **John**, an eagle.

Evening Prayer. Now the common English designation, borrowed from the *Book of Common Prayer*, for the office of prayer at sunset, formerly in the Roman Catholic and Lutheran churches called VESPERS.

Evensong. The name used in Sweden and in England for Evening Prayer (VESPERS).

Ewer (YOU-er; Middle English from Latin *aquarius*, relating to water). A large metal (usually brass) pitcher used to carry water to the baptismal font.

Ex opere operantis (ex OH-per-ay OH-pear-an-tiss; Latin, from the work of the worker). A term used to indicate that the effects of sacraments and sacramentals depend upon the faith and love for God with which the action or object is employed.

Ex opere operato (ex OH-per-ay OH-pear-ah-toe; Latin, from the work performed). A term first found in the thirteenth century to express the objective character of a sacrament, indicating that grace is conveyed through the elements by virtue of the rite performed; not that the sacrament is a mere sign that grace has already been given, or that the sacrament stimulates the faith of the recipient and thus occasions the receipt of grace, or that what determines the effect is the virtue of either the minister or the recipient of the sacrament.

Ex voto (Latin, out of devotion). A tablet or small painting placed in a church expressing gratitude to a saint.

Exaudi (ex-OW-dee; Latin, Hear [O Lord, when I cry with my voice]). The name given in medieval missals and in Lutheran use to the Sunday after the Ascension, from the first word of the INTROIT for the day.

Excommunication (Middle English from Latin *excommunicatus*, put out of the community). Exclusion from the communion of the church, deriving from Matthew 18:15-18 and Matthew 16:19; also John 20:23. Churches of the Reformation have emphasized excommunication as a form of pastoral care rather than as an assertion of ecclesiastical authority. (See the exhortation to communicants in the Order for Public Confession in the *Common Service Book.*) By the nineteenth century there was little possibility of meaningful church discipline except in the most extreme cases.

Exhortation (Middle English from Latin *exhortari*, to encourage). A liturgical address to the congregation; specifically, the address to communicants in many Lutheran church orders which preserved and redirected some of the themes of the discarded CANON.

Exomologesis (eks-OM-ol-oh-GEEt-sis; Greek, confession). The whole process of reconciliation, including the confession of sins, satisfaction, and absolution, by which a penitent is restored to the communion of the church.

Exorcism (EK-sore-sizz-em; Middle English from Greek *exorkizein*, to drive out an evil spirit by means of an oath). The cleansing of a candidate for Holy Baptism by driving out Satan and unclean spirits to make room for the Holy Spirit.

Exorcism Sunday. The third Sunday in Lent, called OCULI in medieval calendars or *Dominica exorcismi*, the exorcisms being performed to prepare candidates for baptism at Easter.

Exposition (Middle English from Latin *expositus*, set out). 1. The explanation of passages of Scripture. 2. The exhibition of the consecrated host of the Eucharist for adoration by the congregation. See MONSTRANCE.

Exsultet (ek-SULL-tet; Latin, rejoice). The Easter Proclamation (PRAECONIUM) in the Easter Vigil, sung by a deacon. It is perhaps the most noteworthy text in the entire liturgy.

Extreme unction. The sacramental action now called Anointing of the Sick. The older name derives from the anointing of the extremities of the body—eyes, nose, ears, mouth, hands, feet—and was only received when one was near death, the emphasis on healing having been largely lost.

Exultavit cor meum (ek-sull-TAHV-it core MAY-um; Latin, My heart rejoices). A song of Hannah (1 Samuel 2:1-10), given as Canticle 7 in the *Common Service Book* and the *Service Book and Hymnal* and as the canticle in Morning Prayer on Wednesday of Week II in the Liturgy of the Hours.

Eye. An all-seeing eye—a rather disconcerting item in church ornamentation, usually enclosed within an equilateral triangle—represents the penetrating gaze of God "unto whom all hearts are open, all desires known, and from whom no secrets are hid." The eye may also be understood, more comfortably, as signifying God's watchful care, as in Psalm 33:18.

Ff

Fair linen (Old English, clean, spotless linen). The topmost cloth of fine linen that covers the top of the altar and hangs down at either end. It usually looks best when it is of generous proportions and hangs nearly to the floor. It is commonly embroidered with five white crosses, in the center and at each of the corners of the mensa, to represent the five wounds of Jesus (hands, feet, and side), since the fair linen is often explained as representing the winding sheet in which the body of Jesus was wrapped when it was taken down from the cross.

Faldstool (FALLD-stool; medieval Latin *faldistolium*, a folding stool). 1. A light, backless chair, used by bishops for confirmations and ordinations, and sometimes by other clergy. 2. A PRIE-DIEU.

Fall (Old English, to drop). A term used to designate the pendant paraments on the altar, pulpit, and lectern.

Fan (Old English from Latin *vannus*, a fan). 1. At least from the fourth century, fans were occasionally used at the Eucharist to keep insects away; the practice continued in the West into the fourteenth century. Their use continues in the Eastern church in fanning the Holy Gifts, suggesting the hovering presence of the seraphim; such fans are called **ripidia** (singular **ripidion**), each a round metal disk on a wooden pole, painted with an image of the six-winged seraphim. 2. When the pope was carried in procession on a SEDIA GESTATORIA, two fans were used as a mark of honor. The fans were called by their Latin name *flabella*, singular *flabellum*.

Fanon (FAN-en; Middle English from Old French *fanon*, fabric). 1. An embroidered cloth, especially a MANIPLE, but also an OFFERTORY VEIL, a HUMERAL VEIL, a BANNER, or a piece of silk attached to a bishop's CROZIER. 2. A striped scarflike vestment worn by the pope when celebrating solemn high mass, a papal AMICE, formerly called an ORALE.

Farse (FARCE; Middle English from Latin *farcire*, to stuff). To expand or fill out a liturgical text, generally in connection with its musical setting, by adding or interpolating words or phrases. The KYRIE has most commonly suffered this treatment.

Fasola (fa-SO-la; from the notes fa, sol, la). The singing school SHAPE

NOTE movement at the end of the eighteenth century into the first third of the nineteenth century, particularly in rural Appalachia and especially in the South, which had a great influence on the development of collections of sacred song such as the *Repository of Sacred Music* (1813), *Kentucky Harmony* (1816), and *Southern Harmony* (1835).

Fast (Old English *faestan*, to observe, to fast). 1. Abstinence from food as a religious discipline. More specifically, in recent Roman Catholic use meat was forbidden on days of ABSTINENCE, but no restriction was placed on the quantity of food that may be eaten; on days of **fasting** the quantity was also restricted. The ancient fast days, dating from the *DIDACHE*, were Wednesday (the day of the Lord's betrayal) and Friday (the day of his crucifixion). 2. A day, time, or season of fasting.

Fasten's Eve. A name in Scotland for SHROVE TUESDAY.

Fastnacht (German, fast night). A name in Germany for SHROVE TUESDAY.

Feast (Middle English from Latin *festus*, joyful, festal). A joyful holy day commemorating an event or person. In current Roman Catholic use, a feast (*festa*) is a holy day ranking between a SOLEMNITY and a MEMORIAL, characterized by the use of the GLORIA IN EXCELSIS but not the creed.

Feast of Fools. A saturnalian celebration of temporary release from restraint and decorum, consisting of the election of a boy bishop, a parody of the mass, the use of foul-smelling incense, and general roughhouse in the churches. Such celebrations took place at Christmas time, most often on Holy Innocents' Day (December 28) or St. Stephen's Day (December 26). They were banned by the Synod of Toledo in 1473.

Feast of the title. The celebration of the event or mystery for which a church is named when the name is not that of a saint (in which case the celebration is called the **patronal festival** or **feast**). Thus the feast of the title of Holy Cross Church is September 14, Holy Cross Day.

Felix culpa (FAY-liks COOL-pa; Latin, happy sin). A phrase from the EXSULTET, expressing the paradox of the fortunate fall, that human sin elicited still greater love from God than that expressed in creation: had it not been for the fall of humanity into sin, there would have been no need for the revelation of the Redeemer.

Fencing the table. Restricting access to the Holy Communion by forbidding such as those not confirmed, those living in open sin, or those not members of a particular parish to come to the altar. Liturgically such restriction is declared in the Eastern liturgies by the priest's cry at the conclusion of the liturgy of the word, "Depart, all catechumens; let no catechumen remain"; in Western churches the restriction is sometimes made literal by closing a gate in the altar rail.

Ferial (FEH-ree-al; Latin *feria*, weekday). Weekday, as opposed to Sunday or festival; **feria** are days that are neither a FEAST nor a FAST.

Fermentum (fer-MEN-tum; Latin, leaven). In fifth-century Rome, fragments of the eucharistic bread from the papal Sunday mass were sent to the surrounding parish churches to be mixed in the chalice to indicate the unity of the eucharistic celebrations. The custom survived in a modified form in the MAUNDY Thursday liturgy until the eighth century.

Fiddle-back. The derisive name applied to eighteenth-century CHA-SUBLES because of their violin-shaped cut: shortened and narrowed with the resulting front and back panels indented on each side so as not to impede the movement of the arms.

Filioque (Latin, and from the Son). The formula expressing the double procession of the Holy Spirit from the Father and from the Son, added by the Western church to the Nicene-Constantinopolitan Creed beginning at the Third Council of Toledo in 589 and adopted at Rome shortly after A.D. 1000. It became a major contributing factor to the divi-sion between the Eastern church, which rejects the phrase, and the Western church.

Finial (Middle English variant of final). The decorated top of a pinnacle.

Fire. Tongues of flame, usually seven for the seven gifts of the Spirit, represent the manifestation of the Holy Spirit on the Day of Pentecost.

Fire, blessing of new. See BLESSING OF THE NEW FIRE.

First Vespers. The beginning of an important festival, celebrated on its eve at sundown, marking the beginning of the day as in Genesis 1; called in present Roman Catholic use Evening Prayer I. The festival then concludes with second Vespers on the day itself. Thus first Vespers of the Epiphany is celebrated on January 5 and second Vespers on January 6.

Fish. The letters of the Greek word *ichthus* form a rebus, which represents *J*esus *CH*rist *G*od's (*theou*) *S*on (*uios*), the *S*avior (*soter*). Fish were also an ancient symbol of life and reproduction.

Five. See NUMBER SYMBOLISM.

Fixed festivals. Feasts of the Christian calendar attached to specific dates (Christmas, Epiphany, saints' days), in contrast to those festivals that are MOVEABLE, such as Easter and Pentecost.

Flabellum, flabella. See FAN.

Flagon (Middle English from Latin *flasco*, a bottle, flask). A pitcher, usually made of silver, in which the wine is kept before being poured into the CHALICE during Holy Communion.

Fleche (French, an arrow). A light, slender spire set on the roofline, generally at the center of the CROSSING.

Fleur-de-lis (FLER-de-LEE; Middle English from Old French, lily flower). A stylized form of the lily, a symbol of purity and virginity, and hence a symbol of the Virgin Mary. Because of its three (although unequal) lobes, it is sometimes understood as a symbol of the Holy Trinity.

Flowers. Only genuine flowers are appropriate for the adornment of an altar and the church. Christianity eschews all deception and falsity. The placing of flowers, especially on great festivals, should never obstruct the clear view of and access to the altar. The use of flowers is to be discouraged during Lent.

Font (Old English from Latin *fons*, a spring, fountain). A basin or tank of metal or stone designed to hold water for the administration of Holy Baptism.

Font, blessing of the. See BLESSING OF THE FONT.

Food, blessing of. See BLESSING OF FOOD AT EASTER.

Fools, Feast of. See FEAST OF FOOLS.

Footpace (foot, Old English; pace, Middle English from Latin *passus*, a step). The raised platform or top step on which the altar is built. Also called a PREDELLA.

Forel (FOR-el; Middle English, a case, from Old French, sheath). A BURSE.

Forma ac ratio (Latin, form and reason). A liturgy based on Calvin's work, drafted by Johannes a Lasco (Jan Laski, 1499-1560) for German refugees living in London.

Formula missae (MISS-eye; Latin, formula of the mass). Luther's Formula of Mass and Communion (1523), a revision and simplification of the Roman *Ordo missae*. It is not itself a liturgical text but rather a commentary on the existing Latin mass text.

Forty hours devotion (Quadrantore or **quarantore)**. A modern Catholic devotion to the Blessed Sacrament, begun in Italy in the sixteenth century, in which the consecrated HOST is exposed for forty hours, during which the faithful pray before it by turns throughout this time. A solemn mass begins and closes the devotion.

Fraction (Middle English from Latin *fractio*, the breaking). The breaking of the bread in the Holy Communion to prepare the bread for distribution.

Frontal (Middle English from Latin *frons*, the front, forehead). A PARAMENT, usually in the color of the season, which covers the entire front of an altar. Sometimes called for clarity a **full frontal**. It is a most welcome addition to the furnishings of a church, making a bold statement by its color and helping to focus attention on the altar, the center of the church's action. See also JACOBEAN FRONTAL.

Frontlet. A narrow band, usually in the liturgical color of the season, which extends across the top front of an altar. Also called a SUPER-FRONTAL, although some dislike the term since the frontlet is often used without a frontal beneath it, primarily for reasons of economy.

Gg

Gallery (Middle English from Latin *galeria*, a porch). 1. A roofed promenade, especially one extending along the wall of a building and supported by arches on the outer side. 2. An upper floor, projecting from one or more walls, above the main floor of a large building or church to accommodate additional people.

Gallican (GAL-i-can). Pertaining to the USE of France (Gaul). The other great Western liturgy besides the Roman rite, characterized by florid style, sometimes understood to be a family including the AMBROSIAN and the MOZARABIC rites, which existed for centuries in the Western church until it was suppressed by Charlemagne ca. 800.

Galloon (gah-LOON; French *galon*, to decorate with ribbons). An ornamental tape or narrow ribbon commonly made of metallic thread or embroidery, used as an edging or other decoration on paraments and vestments.

Gargoyle (GAR-goil; Middle English from Old French *gargouille*, throat). A roof spout carved to represent a grotesque figure of a human or a beast and projected from a gutter to carry rainwater away from the wall. Delightful examples of medieval whimsy, these figures can be understood to symbolize evil being expelled by the Gospel.

Gaudete (GOW-de-tay; Latin, rejoice). The third Sunday in Advent, the name being derived from the first word of the medieval Latin INTROIT. The Sunday was thus seen as a parallel to the fourth Sunday in Lent, LAETARE, with its temporary lessening of the solemnity of the season.

Gelasian sacramentary (gell-ASIAN). A Vatican manuscript of the mid-eighth century, the oldest known Roman sacramentary in which the feasts are ordered according to the church year. Its attribution to Pope Gelasius (492-496) is mistaken.

Gelineau (GHEL-in-oh). A method of singing psalms and canticles to melodic formulas, characterized by a regular recurring pulse that is subdivided to accommodate a variable number of syllables in a manner approximating speech rhythms, developed by Joseph Gelineau in France in the twentieth century.

Geneva gown. See GOWN.

Genuflection (Latin *genu*, the knee, and *flectare*, to bend). Touching the right knee to the ground as an act of adoration, made at such times as entering a church, passing an altar or (from the fourteenth century) the reserved Sacrament, and (from the eleventh century) at the words in the NICENE CREED *incarnatus est* ("and was made man" or "and became truly human").

Girdle (Old English *gyrdel*, an enclosure). A long white cotton rope tied around the waist to keep an ALB in place. Also called a CINCTURE. It is no longer a necessary part of the vestments.

Gloria in excelsis (GLOR-ee-ah in ex-CHEL-sis; Latin, Glory [to God] in the highest). The greater doxology; a canticle based on the song of the angels in Luke 2:14. It originated in the Eastern services of daily prayer (it is Canticles 6 and 20 in Morning Prayer in the 1979 *Book of Common Prayer*) and became the principal hymn of praise in the Western Eucharist beginning in the sixth century.

Gloria, laus, et honor (Latin, Glory, laud, and honor). The hymn by Theodolph of Orleans (ca. 780-821) known in English in John Mason Neale's translation, "All glory, laud, and honor," sung during the procession with palms on the Sunday of the Passion.

Gloria Patri (Latin, glory to the Father). The lesser doxology, used to conclude ANTIPHONAL PSALMODY and to serve as an ascription of praise and confession of the Holy Trinity at the beginning of Morning Prayer. The older form of this doxology, "Glory to the Father, and to the Son, and to the Holy Spirit," without the later addition, "as it was in the beginning, is now, and will be forever," is preserved in many RESPONSORIES.

Gloria tibi (TIB-ee; Latin, Glory to you). The acclamation sung or said in response to the announcement of the reading of the Holy Gospel, "Glory to you, O Lord."

Glossary (Middle English from Latin *glossa*, a word that needs explanation, from Greek *glossa*, tongue, language). A collection of glosses, definitions of terms, the explanation of the jargon of a field or profession. It affords the opportunity for comment as well as definition, indeed the airing of prejudices and opinions to the edification and entertainment of readers.

Golden number (Old English). Meton, the Athenian astronomer, in 432 B.C. found that 235 lunar months very nearly equal nineteen solar years, and this calculation was adopted by the Christian church in calculating the date of Easter. The golden number is found by adding one to the number of the year and dividing by nineteen; the remainder is the golden number of the year in question or, if there is no remainder, the golden number is nineteen. The number is called "golden" because of its value in calculating the date of Easter.

Golden rose. An award, originally a golden flower or spray, blessed on Laetare, the fourth Sunday in Lent, given by the pope to churches, governments, cities, rulers, and others of distinction for service to the Holy See.

Good Friday (Middle English, apparently from God's Friday). Friday in Holy Week, the annual commemoration of the crucifixion, to be understood as part of the unified celebration of the passion, death, and resurrection of Christ, the sacred TRIDUUM.

Good Shepherd Sunday. The fourth Sunday of Easter on which the Gospel for all three years of the lectionary cycle presents the image of Christ the Good Shepherd. Before the calendar reform begun in 1969, the image of the Good Shepherd occurred in the readings for the second Sunday after Easter, MISERICORIDA DOMINI.

Gospel (GOSS-pul; Middle English from Old English *Godspell*, good news, translating Latin *evangelium*). 1. The good news of what God has done through the death and resurrection of Christ, rescuing, renewing, and remaking the world; the treasure of the church and its central and essential proclamation. 2. The LECTION from one of the four Gospels appointed for the Eucharist, understood as the contemporary proclamation of the words and deeds of Christ among his people who hear the reading.

Gospel book (Middle English from Old English *Godspell*, good news, translating Latin *evangelium*). An ornately bound and decorated volume containing the Gospels to be read at the Eucharist. Also called the Book of the Gospels.

Gospel canticle. A fixed New Testament song appointed for Morning Prayer (BENEDICTUS), Evening Prayer (MAGNIFICAT), and Compline (NUNC DIMITTIS), so called because it is drawn from St. Luke's Gospel and is itself a statement and proclamation of the good news.

Gospel side. The liturgically NORTH side of the SANCTUARY, the right side as one faces the congregation, hence the place of honor second only to the altar itself, and the place from which the GOSPEL was read in the mass of the Middle Ages.

Gospeller (Middle English from Old English *Godspellere*). The minister assigned to read the Gospel in the Eucharist; traditionally one who has been ordained (to the office of deacon).

Gown (Middle English from Latin *gunna*, robe, fur). A loose black robe with wide sleeves worn as a preaching gown by Reformed ministers; sometimes called a **Geneva gown**. In English ritualistic controversies its use was understood to represent the preaching of the word over against the eucharistic celebration represented by the Anglican SURPLICE.

Graded cross. See CROSS.

Gradine (gray-DEAN; Latin *gradus*, a step). A steplike shelf behind an altar in the EASTWARD POSITION, that is, against or near the EAST wall, on which are placed crucifix or cross, candles, flowers. Also called a RETABLE.

Gradual (GRAD-you-al; Middle English from Latin *gradus*, a step). A liturgical anthem consisting of verses of psalms arranged according to a special form, which was sung between the EPISTLE and the GOSPEL, a vestige of the RESPONSORIAL PSALMODY, now restored, sung between the first and second lessons. The name derives from the step (*gradus*) of the AMBO from which the gradual was sung. See also GRADUALE.

Graduale (grad-you-AHL-ay). A service book containing the proper choir music for the choir at mass. The *Graduale Romanum* provides for Sundays and feasts an INTROIT, GRADUAL (in Lent a TRACT), OFFERTORY, and COMMUNION. The book is sometimes called the Gradual.

Grapes. 1. Shown with stalks of wheat, grapes signify the Holy Communion. 2. On a vine, they signify Christ the vine and his disciples. 3. Shown carried on a pole, they signify the promised land (Numbers 13:21-24).

Great Amen. (Old English *great*, thick, coarse). The congregation's sung or spoken affirmation of the GREAT THANKSGIVING proclaimed by the presiding minister.

Great Entrance. In the Eastern church, the solemn procession in which the bread and wine are carried from the **prothesis** (a table of preparation on the left side of the APSE) out through the ICONOSTASIS into the view of the congregation and up to the altar for the offertory.

Great Hallel. Psalm 136. See HALLEL.

Great Octave. Easter as an OCTAVE, made of eight Sundays (Easter Day through the Day of Pentecost) instead of the consecutive days of one week; the week of weeks, a week composed of seven weeks rather than seven days; the Fifty Days of Easter.

Great Sabbath. Saturday in Holy Week, so called from John 19:31.

Great Thanksgiving. An ancient name, recently recovered, for the ANAPHORA, that prayer which begins with the PREFACE verses, continues with the preface, SANCTUS, eucharistic prayer (and/or the VERBA in Lutheran use), and concludes with the GREAT AMEN.

Great Week. The name given in the early church to Holy Week, St. Augustine explained, because of the great things that it commemorates.

Greek cross. See CROSS.

Green. The neutral liturgical color, used in "ordinary time" after the Epiphany and after Pentecost and sometimes explained as representing growth in the knowledge and love of God.

Gregorian chant (greg-OR-ee-an). The historic liturgical song of the Western church, unison and unaccompanied, for soloists (CANTORS), choirs, and congregations; used for psalms and canticles, hymns, readings, and liturgical texts. It is named for Gregory the Great (Bishop of Rome, 590-604), although it existed earlier. Also called PLAINCHANT or Plainsong.

Gregorian sacramentary. A family of sacramentaries ascribed to Pope Gregory I (590-604) and containing elements composed by him. Ca. 790, Pope Hadrian I sent Charlemagne a sacramentary, the *Hadrianum*, which he described as the work of Gregory. The book was not complete and was supplemented by Gelasian material. The Roman missal is the result of the combination of these two sources.

Gremial (GREM-ee-al; Latin *gremium*, the lap). An apron placed upon the bishop's lap when seated during the Eucharist.

Habit (Middle English from Latin *habere*, to possess). The distinctive clothing worn by a particular person or group at regular or agreed upon times. Thus, for example, the choir habit is the dress of those who pray daily prayer in the CHOIR of a church: CASSOCK and SURPLICE.

Hagioscope (HAY-gee-oh-scope; Greek *hagios*, holy, and *skopein*, to see). An oblique opening in an interior wall of a church to make it possible for people in obscured places, such as a TRANSEPT, to have a view of the altar. Also called a **squint**.

Hail Mary. See AVE MARIA.

Hallel (ha-LAIL; Hebrew, song of praise). A name given to Psalms 113-118 because of the recurring word *Hallelujah;* used during Passover, originally during the killing of the Passover lambs, and sometimes therefore called the Egyptian Hallel to distinguish it from the Great Hallel, Psalm 136. The Hallel is probably "the hymn" referred to in the accounts of the Last Supper (Matthew 26:30; Mark 14:26): Psalm 113-114 sung before the Passover meal, Psalm 115-118 after it.

Hallelujah (Hebrew, praise the Lord). In the liturgy, except in the psalter, the ancient shout is usually found in its Greek form, ALLELUIA.

Halo (Greek *halos*, the disk of the sun or moon). A luminous ring or disk of light surrounding heads or bodies of sacred figures. See NIMBUS.

Hammer. Shown with nails as a symbol of the passion of Christ.

Hanc igitur (hanc IG-i-toor; Latin, [accept] therefore this [offering]). The fourth prayer of the Roman CANON, a later addition attributed in part to Gregory the Great, and beginning, "Therefore, Lord, we pray you to accept this offering of our service. . . ."

Hand. In church ornamentation shown reaching down, a symbol of God offering protection and help; upright with the thumb and first two fingers extended, a symbol of blessing from the triune God.

Hangings (Old English *hangian*, to hang, suspend). Another and less specifically churchly name ("hanging" is used of any drapery) for the PARAMENTS, so called because they hang from the altar, pulpit, and lectern.

Harmony (Middle English from Greek *harmonia*, agreement, harmony). That system of musical composition by which simultaneous musical tones are arranged and related to form chords that are "consonant"; contrasted with melody and COUNTERPOINT.

Harp. A symbol of music, especially the strains of heaven (Revelation 14:1-3; 15:2-4).

Hassock (HASS-ek; Old English *hassuc*, a clump of matted vegetation). A thick cushion for kneeling. Because a hassock is individually adjusted, it is preferable to sliding kneeling benches.

Hearse or **Herse** (HURSE; Middle English from Latin *hirpex*, a harrow, rake). A harrow-shaped, triangular frame for holding candles, placed over the bier at a funeral, on which epitaphs were once hung; the triangular stand for holding the fifteen candles used at TENEBRAE.

Heart. A symbol of Christian charity (1 Corinthians 13:13).

Heortology (HAY-or-toll-a-gee; Greek *heorte*, feast, and *logos*, study). The study of the days and seasons of the church year, their origin, meaning, and observance.

High altar (Old English). The principal ALTAR of a church having more than one altar; so called from its being raised above the level of the nave.

High mass (*missa solemnis*). The celebration of the Eucharist with deacon and subdeacon assisting the celebrant, accompanied by a choir, servers, and incense. In Roman Catholic use, since the Second Vatican Council the term no longer appears. In Sweden and elsewhere, especially in the Anglican church, it remains as the regular term for the sung celebration of Holy Communion.

History of the Passion. A harmony of the accounts of Jesus' passion given in the four Gospels. At the time of the Reformation, Bugenhagen arranged such a history that was most influential. The practice descended from the medieval *Passionales*, which divided the passion history for devotional purposes, the portions not always following the account of a particular Gospel but taken from one or another as seemed appropriate. A History of the Passion appeared in the *Church Book* (1868), the *Common Service Book*, and the text edition of the *Service Book and Hymnal* (1967). With the understanding in modern biblical scholarship of the separate point of view of each of the four Gospels, such a harmony is no longer thought desirable.

Holy Communion. 1. The celebration of the EUCHARIST. The title of the principal service of the church in the *Lutheran Book of Worship* and in earlier editions of the *Book of Common Prayer*. 2. The reception of the consecrated bread and wine.

Holy Cross, feasts of the. The present Holy Cross Day (in the Roman rite called the Triumph of the Cross), September 14, derives from the earlier feast of the Exaltation of the Holy Cross, commemorating the exposition of the cross in Jerusalem in 629 by Emperor Heraclius after he had recovered it from the Persians. A secondary feast on May 3 commemorated the finding of the holy cross by St. Helena, called the Invention (Latin *invenire,* to find) of the Cross.

Holy day. A day on the liturgical calendar specified for particular observance, such as the commemoration of a saint.

Holy Door. The central opening in an ICONOSTASIS of a Byzantine church building, the Royal Gate through which the holy gifts, the consecrated bread and wine, are brought to commune the people.

Holy Family. The feast in honor of Jesus, Mary, and Joseph, celebrated on the Roman calendar on the Sunday within the octave of Christmas; established in 1893.

Holy Innocents. The feast on December 28, introduced in the fourth century in the East, to commemorate the innocent children killed by King Herod in his desire to do away with the infant Christ.

Holy orders. 1. The sacrament of ordination by which candidates are admitted to the ministry of the church. 2. The principal orders of clergy in Christian churches: bishops, presbyters, deacons, subdeacons, readers. 3. John Donne understood the term to mean the orders or commands under which ministers of the church were sent to preach the word and administer the sacraments.

Holy Saturday. The Saturday in Holy Week, Easter Eve, the principal liturgy of which is the Easter Vigil.

Holy Thursday. 1. Thursday in Holy Week, Maundy Thursday, on which the sacred TRIDUUM begins with the evening celebration of the Lord's Supper. 2. Especially in England, Ascension Day, the fortieth day after Easter.

Holy Trinity. Trinity Sunday, the Sunday after Pentecost, introduced early in the tenth century; the feast was immensely popular throughout northern Europe (hence the popularity of Trinity as the title of Lutheran and Anglican churches) and was established throughout the Western church in 1334.

Holy water. Water blessed to serve as a reminder of baptism.

Holy Week. The seven days commemorating the passion of Christ, beginning with the Sunday of the Passion and continuing until the Easter Vigil. See GREAT WEEK.

Holy Year. A year of jubilee in the Roman church in which the pope grants special indulgences to pilgrims. Since 1470, a holy year is celebrated every twenty-five years.

Homilist. A pretentious name for one more straightforwardly and simply called a preacher, used by those uncomfortable with the informal Protestant connotations of the traditional name.

Homily (HOMM-i-lee; Middle English from Greek *homilia*, conversation, discourse). A sermon on a biblical text, an exposition of Scripture.

Horns of the altar. The corners of the altar, taken from Psalm 118:27. The Gospel horn is the liturgically northwest corner (left front facing the altar); the epistle horn is the southwest corner (right front).

Hosanna (Hebrew, save now). The ancient shout of victory appears in the liturgy in the SANCTUS.

Host (Middle English from Latin *hostia*, an animal slain in sacrifice). The bread used in the Holy Communion when it is in the form of a wafer, conveying to the communicant the Lamb of God, slain to take away the sin of the world. A large wafer, called a **priest's host,** is used by the presiding minister during the consecration because it is more easily seen by the congregation.

Hours (Middle English from Latin and Greek *hora*, time, season). The various services of the daily prayer of the church; the canonical hours which, taken together, comprise the Liturgy of the Hours.

Houseling cloth (HOUSE-ling; Old English *husl*, the Eucharist, probably originally an offering). A white linen cloth which vests the altar rail in Swedish churches. It was originally a long cloth spread or held by communicants at the reception of the Sacrament; still the custom in Eastern churches, replaced in 1929 in the Roman Catholic church by a plate of precious metal.

Humeral veil (HUE-mer-al; Latin *humerus*, upper arm, shoulder). A long, wide scarf of rich material worn over the shoulders and hands of a minister who solemnly carries the consecrated elements of the Holy Communion; in the past, worn by the subdeacon in the celebration of mass.

Hymn (Middle English from Greek *hymnos*, a festal song to the gods or heroes). In the Septuagint the term is applied to the psalms; used in the Pauline writings for Christian songs (Ephesians 5:19; Colossians 3:16).

Hymn of the Day. In the *Lutheran Book of Worship*, the principal congregational song during the Eucharist; sung following the sermon, properly setting forth a principal theme of the readings and sermon. In European Lutheran practice, particular hymns are commonly assigned to the Sundays and feasts of the year, forming a kind of PROPER for use by the congregation.

Hymn of Praise. In the *Lutheran Book of Worship*, the GLORIA IN EXCELSIS or WORTHY IS CHRIST sung as part of the entrance rite.

Icon (EYE-con; Greek *eikon*, likeness, image). A two-dimensional picture, painted under strict theological prescriptions including spiritual preparation by the artist; used in the Eastern church instead of three-dimensional images to avoid breaking the second commandment (the third in Protestant, but not Lutheran, numbering) against graven images.

Iconostasis (eye-con-oh-STASS-iss). A screen ornamented with icons of the saints which, in Eastern churches, separates the holy place with the altar, the BEMA, from the congregation, corresponding to the chancel rail in many Western churches. It is pierced by three doors: the central Royal Gate or Holy Door flanked by icons of Christ to the right and the THEOTOKOS to the left, the northern door through which the GREAT ENTRANCE comes on its way to the altar, and the southern door. The icons which cover the screen represent those who dwell in heaven and surround the holy place.

IHS or **IHC.** The first three letters of the name Jesus in Greek, IHC being the older form. It is often misunderstood by those who know no Greek as an abbreviation for "In his steps."

Illatio (ill-AHT-see-oh; Latin, the action of bringing into a place, an offering). A name in certain Gallican and Spanish missals for the PREFACE; also CONTESTATIO or IMMOLATIO.

Illuminandi (il-lume-in-AHN-dee; Latin, enlightened). An ancient name for those about to be baptized.

Illumination (Latin *illuminare*, to light up). The art of adorning texts of manuscripts with colors and drawings; initial letters were most often the special subjects of such honor.

Immaculate Conception. The celebration on December 8 of the conception of the Virgin Mary, without the stain of original sin, in her mother's womb. The feast has its origin in the seventh century in the East. The doctrine, not defined as a dogma in the West until 1857, is accepted by the Lutheran Confessions, although it was opposed by the great devotee of Mary, Bernard of Clairvaux.

Immersion (Latin *immergere*, to dip). A method of baptism, used at least from the second century, in which the candidate stood in water while more water was poured over the head. See AFFUSION, SUBMERSION.

Immolatio (im-o-LAT-see-oh; Latin, a sacrifice, immolation). A name in certain French and Spanish missals for the PREFACE; also CONTESTATIO or ILLATIO.

Improperia (im-pro-PAY-ree-a; from Latin *improbare*, to disapprove, reject). The REPROACHES.

In coena Domini (in KAY-na DOM-in-ee; Latin, at the supper of the Lord). A papal bull declaring a general excommunication of all heretics, read at the Maundy Thursday mass in the fifteenth and sixteenth centuries; the custom lingered in some places until the eighteenth century.

In illo tempore (in ILL-oh TEM-po-ray; Latin, at that time). The traditional introductory formula for the Gospel reading, directing the hearers' attention to the primordial formative time when the definitive essence of Christianity was established, giving meaning to all succeeding ages.

In Paradisum (par-a-DEE-sum; Latin, into paradise). An anthem, probably of Gallican origin, dating from at least the tenth century, used in medieval funeral rites to accompany the procession to the church or to the grave: "Into paradise may the angels lead you. . . ."

Incarnatus est (in-car-NAH-tus). The phrase in the NICENE CREED confessing the incarnation of Jesus Christ, translated in English "and was made man" or "and became truly human." In the Western church it has been the custom to GENUFLECT or to bend the head and shoulders in a profound bow at these words, in token of Christ's humility.

Incense (Middle English from Latin *incendere*, to set on fire). Fragrant smoke, a symbol of prayer used in Jewish worship in the Temple and mentioned in Revelation 8:3-5. The first clear evidence of its use in Christian worship is ca. 500.

Ingressa (in-GRESS-a; Latin, entrance). The entrance rite.

I.N.I. Abbreviation of the Latin *in nomine iesu*, in the name of Jesus.

I.N.R.I. Abbreviation of the Latin inscription placed above the cross of Jesus: *Jesus Nazarenus rex Judaeorum*, Jesus of Nazareth, King of the Jews. James Joyce in *Ulysses* records a mistaken interpretation by school children who knew no Latin, "Iron nails ran in."

Intercession (Old French from Latin *intercedere*, to come between). Prayer on behalf of others. The principal place of intercession in the Eucharist is at the close of the liturgy of the word before the offertory, which begins the liturgy of the table; other intercessions are offered in the Lutheran Kyrie (an abbreviated Eastern deacon's litany) and sometimes at the conclusion of the GREAT THANKSGIVING before the doxology and GREAT AMEN.

Intinction (Latin *intingere*, to dip in). Dipping an edge of the HOST into the wine in the chalice and thus administering the consecrated bread and wine together to the communicant. Its first use was apparently with the sick for ease of consumption. The practice was forbidden by the Council of Braga in 675 but was reintroduced in the eleventh century. It had virtually disappeared by 1200 until it was revived by the Anglicans. In 1965 it was approved by the Roman Catholic church as one of the ways of receiving Holy Communion under both KINDS.

Intone (Middle English from Latin *intonare*, to utter in a musical tone). To recite in a singing voice, to chant.

Introit (in-TROW-it; Middle English from Latin *introire*, to enter). The liturgical anthem consisting of an ANTIPHONAL psalm with ANTIPHON and GLORIA PATRI, sung as the entrance song of the mass. In the Middle Ages the psalm shrunk to but one verse when its function as an entrance hymn was largely lost.

Invitatory (in-VYE-ta-tory; Middle English from Latin *invitare*, to invite). An invitation to praise, used as an antiphon to the VENITE in Morning Prayer. It is a variable PROPER that changes with the season. Sometimes "invitatory" is used to refer to the invitatory-antiphon and the Venite together, for they function as a single song of invitation, "Come, let us sing to the Lord."

Invocabit (in-vo-KAH-bit; Latin, he will call upon [me]). The name given to the first Sunday in Lent in the medieval Roman missals and in Lutheran use, deriving from the first word of the INTROIT, the first of the propers for the Sunday, "He shall call upon me [and I will answer him]." In the *Common Service Book*, the verb was mistakenly given in the perfect tense, *Invocavit*.

Invocation (Middle English from Latin *invocare*, to call upon). 1. The words "In the name of the Father, and of the Son, and of the Holy Spirit" at the beginning of the Confession, which immediately precedes the service in Lutheran use, calling upon God who in baptism made his people his own. 2. The EPIKLESIS of the GREAT THANKSGIVING and the Thanksgiving in baptism, calling upon God to send the Holy Spirit.

Ite, missa est (EE-tay MISS-a est; Latin). The conclusion of the Roman mass, at least from the eighth century. The meaning is disputed; it seems to mean something like, "Go, it is over," "Go, you are dismissed." The reply is "Thanks be to God."

Jj

Jacobean frontal (from Latin, *Jacobus*, James). Canon 82 of the Anglican Canons of 1603 ordered that the Lord's Table be "covered, in time of Divine Service, with a carpet of silk or other decent stuff, thought meet by the Ordinary of the place." This cloth, sometimes called a Jacobean frontal (after James I, King of Great Britain, 1603-1625) or a **Laudian frontal** (after William Laud, Archbishop of Canterbury, 1633-1645), covered the entire altar down to the floor on all four sides. Such a generous covering remains a sumptuous parament. Outside of service time, the Jacobean frontal was often removed so that an elaborately carved altar might be seen.

James the Elder, James the Less. See APOSTLES' SYMBOLS.

Jerusalem cross. See CROSS.

Jesse tree. A small tree or representation of a tree decorated with symbols portraying the ancestry of Jesus, the descendant of Jesse, the father of David the king, suggested in part by Isaiah 11:1. The custom is a recent innovation, originating apparently in the twentieth century.

John. See APOSTLES' SYMBOLS, EVANGELISTS' SYMBOLS.

Joint Liturgical Group. An ecumenical organization in Great Britain representing nine churches.

Jubilate (YOU-bil-ah-tay; Latin, rejoice). 1. The name of the third Sunday after Easter in medieval missals and Lutheran use, from the first word of the INTROIT, "Make a joyful noise [unto God]." 2. Psalm 100, beginning in Latin *Jubilate Deo*.

Jubilus (YOU-bill-is; Latin, joy). Lengthy continuations and elaborations of the final vowel of the alleluia sung before the Gospel; a predecessor of the SEQUENCE.

Jude. See APOSTLES' SYMBOLS.

Judica (YOU-di-kah; Latin, Judge [me, O God]). The fifth Sunday in Lent in medieval missals and in Lutheran use, deriving from the first word of the proper INTROIT for the day.

70

Kk

Kaddish (KAHD-ish; Aramaic, sanctification). A prayer of doxology used in Jewish worship as an expression of praise and hope.

Kalendar (Middle English from Latin *kalendae*, the day of the new moon and first day of the month). A variant of calendar, used in certain Anglican quarters to give a Latin echo and more churchly flavor than the more common spelling and to indicate a distinction from the secular calendar.

Kalimavkion or **kamilavkion**. The black cylindrical BIRETTA worn in the Eastern church.

Keys. See PETER under APOSTLES' SYMBOLS.

Kind (Old English *cynd*, nature, birth, race). One of the elements in the Holy Communion, as in reception "under one kind," that is, in the form of bread alone without wine (or vice versa).

Kiss of peace. The mutual greeting of communicants as a sign of their unity in Christ (Romans 16:16, 1 Peter 5:14). In the Eastern, Gallican, Mozarabic, Anglican, and Lutheran rites, following Matthew 5:23, the Peace is given before the offerings are gathered and presented; in the Roman and Ambrosian rites (and optionally in the Lutheran rite), it occurs prior to the distribution of communion.

Kneeling (Old English *cneowlian*). The posture of humiliation required of a class of penitents in the early church called *genuflectentes*, who knelt in the WEST end of the nave during the liturgy of the word. Kneeling on Sundays and in daily worship during EASTER was forbidden by the Council of Nicaea in 325.

Kyrie (KEE-ree-ay; Greek, Lord). 1. A threefold, sixfold, or ninefold cry *Kyrie eleison*, "Lord, have mercy," sung at the beginning of the mass, deriving from a separable response to a litany; the middle member of the cry was in the early Middle Ages changed to *Christe eleison*, "Christ, have mercy," to give the acclamation a trinitarian form. 2. In the *Lutheran Book of Worship*, the peace litany of the assisting minister and congregation in the ENTRANCE RITE of the Holy Communion, borrowed from the Eastern rites and beginning "In peace, let us pray to the Lord."

Kyrie Pantokrator (pan-toh-KRAH-tor; Greek, Lord, the Ruler). A Song of Penitence from the Prayer of Manasseh 1-2, 4, 6-7, 11-15, given as Canticle 14 in Morning Prayer, Rite II in the *Book of Common Prayer*.

Lace. Lace was introduced to church use on the continent of Europe during the late sixteenth century at a time when lace was common to men's clothing; it is not uncommon in Slovak and Polish Lutheran churches and in the Roman Catholic church. One rule governs its use: if lace is considered appropriate for the clergy of a particular parish, then it is appropriate on the altar; otherwise, not.

Ladder. A symbol of the passion of Christ, the means by which his body was taken down from the cross, often pictured with a reed and a sponge.

Lady chapel. A CHAPEL dedicated to the Virgin Mary when it is part of a larger church, common in England, usually to the EAST of the high altar.

Laetare (lie-TAR-ay; Latin, rejoice). The name of the fourth Sunday in Lent, mid-Lent, in medieval missals and in Lutheran use, from the first word of the INTROIT for the day, "Rejoice [ye with Jerusalem]." See REFRESHMENT SUNDAY.

Lamb. See AGNUS DEI.

Lammas (LAHM-as; Middle English from Old English *hlaf-maesse*, loaf mass). August 1, originally a harvest festival when bread baked from the season's first ripe grain was consecrated; then in Christian times the Feast of St. Peter's Chains, commemorating the deliverance of Peter from prison, described in Acts 12:1-11.

Lamp (Middle English from Greek *lampas*, a torch). 1. A lamp kept burning in a church to signify the eternal presence of God. See SANCTUARY LIGHT. 2. In certain churches, seven oil lamps or hanging candles are suspended in front of the altar to recall Revelation 4:5. 3. A representation of a lamp may symbolize the word of God, suggested by Psalm 119:105.

Lantern (Middle English from Latin *lanterna*, a lantern, torch). An open tower erected over the CROSSING of a cruciform church to admit light to the crossing below.

Lappet. See MITER.

Last Gospel. John 1:1-14, read at the GOSPEL SIDE of the altar immediately following the blessing at the end of the mass in the Roman rite, until the reforms of the twentieth century (1964). It was originally part of the priest's private devotion after mass, and in the medieval period was brought out to the altar as a congregational act of thanksgiving.

Lauda Sion salvatorem (Latin, Zion, praise the Savior). A SEQUENCE praising the Holy Sacrament, written ca. 1260 by Thomas Aquinas for the feast of CORPUS CHRISTI. It was one of four sequences retained in the Roman missal of 1570. The hymn has appeared in a number of English translations and paraphrases, among which is "Sion, praise thy Savior singing."

Laudian frontal. See JACOBEAN FRONTAL.

Lauds (LAWDS; Latin *laudare*, to praise). Morning Praise, prayer at sunrise, the beginning of the day; with VESPERS, one of the two principal hours of daily prayer. At the Reformation, Lauds was combined with MATINS and parts of PRIME to form the office known by the Anglicans as Morning Prayer (or Mattins) and by the Lutherans as Matins.

Laus cerei (LOUSE cherry-ee; Latin, praise of the candle). A name for the Easter Proclamation, commonly called the EXSULTET.

Laus tibi (TIB-ee; Latin, praise to you). The acclamation sung or said in response to the reading of the Holy Gospel, "Praise to you, O Christ."

Lavabo (la-VAH-bo; Latin, I will wash [my hands in innocence], from Psalm 26:6). 1. The ceremonial washing of the presiding minister's hands after handling the offering plates and CENSER in connection with the OFFERTORY in preparation for the GREAT THANKSGIVING. Since ancient times the action was understood to be symbolic, besides being obviously utilitarian. St. Augustine said, "The water that flows over the tips of our fingers washes away the last traces of our impurities." See WASHING THE HANDS. In the medieval mass, the action was accompanied by the recitation of Psalm 26:6-12. 2. The small bowl, usually made of silver or other precious metal and containing the water for washing the minister's hands, is sometimes called the lavabo.

Lay reader. A layperson who is authorized to read lessons and to preside at such services as do not require the presidency of an ordained person.

Laying on of hands. A manner of blessing used in the Old Testament and followed by Christ and by the church in confirmation and ordination.

Lectern (LEK-turn; Middle English from Latin *legere*, to read). A desk or stand to hold the Bible for public reading. Sometimes a lectern is two- or three- or even four-sided, mounted on a pivot to hold several books, each open to a different lesson, for the convenience of the readers.

Lectio continua (LEK-see-oh con-TIN-oo-ah; Latin, continuous reading). The practice of reading Scripture in church services in a continuous fashion, each lesson taking up where the previous reading concluded, rather than reading selected PERICOPES.

Lection (LEK-shun; Latin *legere*, to read). A reading of Holy Scripture appointed for the services of the church.

Lectionary (LEK-shun-airy). 1. A table of lessons from Holy Scripture for the church year. There is a three-year cycle of lessons for the Eucharist in common use; the *Book of Common Prayer* and the *Lutheran Book of Worship* have a two-year lectionary for use at daily prayer; the *Lutheran Book of Worship* has also a one-year cycle of readings for the Eucharist. 2. A book containing the texts of the lessons for the church year, together with the RESPONSORIAL PSALM and the VERSE before the Gospel.

Lector (LEK-ter; Latin, reader). A reader of a lesson in a service, who gives life to the written word by voicing it. Anciently, one of the minor orders of the ministry, and in the Eastern church still one of the HOLY ORDERS.

Leisen (LIE-sen; German from the contraction of *Kyrieleis*). A body of sacred pre-Reformation German folk hymns, sung in procession and occasionally during mass, in which each stanza concluded with *Kyrie eleison*, Lord, have mercy, often contracted to *Kyrieleis*.

Lent (Middle English *lente*, spring, from Old English *lengten*, to lengthen [daylight]). The forty weekdays before Easter, beginning on ASH WEDNESDAY. Originally a preparation of candidates for baptism and later a penitential period for all the baptized.

Lenten array (Middle English *arayen*, to arrange). Veils of off-white cloth hung during Lent before crosses, pictures, and such images as are not of an architectural character, the purpose of which is to blend the ornaments into the white walls of the interior of the church until Easter comes again. PARAMENTS, VESTMENTS, and DOSSAL are appropriately of the same color.

Leofric collector. The *Codex Exoniensis*, given to Exeter cathedral by Bishop Leofric in the eleventh century, containing an odd collection of poems, hymns, semi-pagan lyrics and elegies, riddles, and sententious verses.

Leofric missal. A MISSAL of the tenth century used in Exeter cathedral in England.

Leonine sacramentary. The earliest surviving collection of prayers according to the Roman rite. The manuscript of the early seventh century, drawing on material from the fifth and sixth centuries, is preserved in Verona, and the sacramentary is sometimes called the **Verona sacramentary**. Its attribution to Leo I (d. 461) is arbitrary, but some of the prayers may indeed be his.

Lex orandi, lex credendi (lex o-RAHN-dee, lex kray-DEN-dee; Latin, the law of praying, the law of believing). An axiom attributed to a lay monk, Prosper of Aquitaine (ca. 390-463), from a capitulum annexed to a letter of Pope Celestine I (422-432) between 435 and 442. In its fuller form, the axiom is *Legem credendi statuat lex orandi* [or *supplicandi*], the rule of prayer determines the rule of faith, implying that the Christian liturgy is the most effective means of preserving and interpreting the faith; or, in anthropological language, creed follows cult.

Libelli (li-BELL-ee; Latin *libelli missarum*, books of masses). Precursors of the sacramentaries, linking the period of free composition and the origin of fixed forms; books containing formularies for masses for a particular period or season for use by a particular church.

Liber commicus (LEE-bear KOMM-i-kus; Latin, excerpt book). A MOZARABIC name for the lectionary, giving complete texts of the PERICOPES. See COMES.

Liber gradualis (grad-you-AL-iss; Latin, book of graduals). A book for the choir, containing the text and music of the GRADUALS sung between the epistle and the Gospel in the medieval mass.

Liber officialis (oh-FISS-ee-AHL-iss; Latin, book of offices). The most significant book by Amalarius of Metz (823) that became the most influential liturgical book of the early Middle Ages in the West, elaborating most ingeniously the allegorical interpretation of the liturgy.

Liber ordinum (OR-din-um; Latin, book of orders, services). A sixth-century Mozarabic book containing a PONTIFICAL, a RITUAL, and some mass texts.

Liber pontificalis (pon-TIFF-i-cal-iss; Latin, book of popes). A collection of early papal biographies possibly begun during the reign of Boniface II (530-532); subsequent editions carried the history down to the fifteenth century.

Liber responsalis (re-spons-AL-iss; Latin, book of responses). A book for the choir, containing its responses and psalms.

Lich gate. See LYCH GATE.

Lichnikon (LICH-ni-kon; Greek, service of light). See LUCERNARIUM.

Lights. The candles on the altar lighted at the celebration of the Holy Communion are called **eucharistic lights**. The candles near the altar lighted for daily prayer are called **office lights**. See VESPER LIGHTS.

Lily. A symbol of virginity and purity and hence associated with the Virgin Mary, especially in representations of the ANNUNCIATION.

Linens. Two kinds of linens are used in the church: **altar linens** consisting of the CERE CLOTH, a protector cloth the exact size of the MENSA, and the FAIR LINEN; and the **sacramental linens** consisting of the CORPORAL, PALL, and PURIFICATORS; the VEIL in Lutheran use is also commonly made of linen.

Lion. 1. A symbol of Christ, the lion of the tribe of Judah (Revelation 5:5). 2. A winged lion symbolizes St. Mark; see EVANGELISTS' SYMBOLS.

Litany (Middle English from Greek *litaneia*, an entreaty). An ancient, highly organized form of intercession with a congregational response to each PREX or to each group of petitions. The two principal litanies are the Eastern deacon's litany, found in the *Lutheran Book of Worship* at the close of Evening Prayer (Vespers) and in an abbreviated form in the Kyrie in the Holy Communion, and in the *Book of Common Prayer* as Form I of the Prayers of the People in the Eucharist; and the Western litany of the saints, found in the *Book of Common Prayer* as the Great Litany deriving from Cranmer's reforms of the Roman litany of the saints, and in the *Lutheran Book of Worship* as the Litany, deriving from Luther's revisions of the Roman litany.

Litany desk. See PRIE-DIEU.

Little Entrance. In the liturgy of the Eastern church, the procession with the Gospel book through the ICONOSTASIS, anticipating and foreshadowing the GREAT ENTRANCE, for the singing of the Holy Gospel before the congregation.

Little Hours. The hours of TERCE, SEXT, and NONE, prayed at nine, noon, and three o'clock. The name derives from the brevity of these hours and their subservience to the principal hours of LAUDS and VESPERS. In the Liturgy of the Hours, the three Little Hours are grouped under the heading of Daytime Prayer (Midmorning, Midday, Midafternoon), and at least one of these is to be prayed by those who cannot pray all three.

Liturgical movement. Practical application of the accumulating knowledge and researches of many disciplines bearing on the origin, development, and meaning of ritual and the church's worship. The movement originated in continental Catholicism in the latter part of the nineteenth century and spread to the Anglican and Lutheran churches and elsewhere.

Liturgy (LIT-ur-gee; Greek *leitourgia*, public service). 1. The body of services of worship of a church. 2. A particular order of service. 3. The Eucharist.

Liturgy of the Hours. The present name in the Roman church for the offices of daily prayer: the Office of Readings (replacing MATINS), Morning Prayer (LAUDS), Daytime Prayer (the LITTLE HOURS), Evening Prayer (VESPERS), and COMPLINE.

Liturgy of SS. Addai and Mari. A Syriac liturgy of Edessa in northeastern Syria, an early center of Christianity. The ANAPHORA is still in use among Nestorian Christians. Notable in this liturgy is the absence of the Institution Narrative, the VERBA.

Liturgy of St. Basil. 1. The Egyptian Coptic liturgy, written originally in Greek. 2. The later Byzantine expansion of the liturgy, still in use in the Orthodox church on certain days. For some centuries, St. Basil was the principal liturgy of Constantinople until it was replaced by the **Liturgy of St. John Chrysostom**, half its length, ca. 1000.

Liturgy of St. James. The liturgy of Jerusalem, widely used until it was suppressed in the twelfth century.

Liturgy of St. John Chrysostom (KRISS-iss-tum). The principal and normal rite of the Orthodox church, having replaced St. Basil (ca. 1000) and probably preserving the form in use in Antioch during St. John Chrysostom's episcopate (370-398).

Liturgy of St. Mark. The liturgy of the patriarchate of Alexandria. The structure of the ANAPHORA is similar to Jewish prayers such as the blessing of food.

Loft (Old English from Old Norse *lopt*, air, attic). A gallery or balcony.

Lord's Day. An ancient designation for the first day of the week (Revelation 1:10), the day of resurrection. The name is probably related to the celebration of the Lord's Supper on that day.

Lorraine, cross of. See CROSS.

Love of St. John. See BLESSING OF WINE.

Low mass. A simplified form of the Eucharist said, not sung, by one priest assisted by one server. In the 1970 Roman *Ordo missae*, the term no longer appears.

Low Sunday. A name for the Sunday following Easter Day, now called the second Sunday of Easter. The origin of the name is unknown; perhaps it simply reflects the contrast with the great solemnity of the preceding feast of Easter Day.

Lucernarium (loo-chair-NAR-ee-um; Latin, service of light). The ceremonial lighting of candles and lamps, which in ancient times marked the time for the beginning of VESPERS and Evening Prayer.

Luke. See EVANGELISTS' SYMBOLS.

Luxeuil lectionary. A seventh-century lectionary used in Paris.

Lych gate or **Lich gate** (Old English *lic*, a corpse). A covered gateway to a churchyard, so arranged as to make it possible to rest a coffin there to await the arrival of the officiating minister and the opening part of the Burial of the Dead.

Lyre. See HARP.

Magi (MAY-jeye; Latin, magicians, astrologers). Another name for the wise men from the East who came to worship the infant Christ as described in Matthew 2. According to tradition there were three of them, representing the three races of humanity, and they bore the names Kaspar or Casper, Melchior, and Balthasar.

Magna et mirabilia (MAHG-na et meer-ah-BILL-ee-a; Latin, great and marvelous [are your deeds, O Lord]). The Song of the Redeemed from Revelation 15:3-4, beginning "O Ruler of the universe, Lord God"; Canticle 19 in Morning Prayer, Rite II in the *Book of Common Prayer* and borrowed as Canticle 21 in the *Lutheran Book of Worship*. In the Liturgy of the Hours it is the canticle in Evening Prayer on Fridays, on the Epiphany and on Pentecost, and on the common of Pastors and on the common of Holy Men.

Magnificat (mahg-NIFF-i-caht; Latin, [my soul] magnifies [the Lord]). The song of Mary from Luke 1:46-55, beginning "My soul proclaims the greatness of the Lord," appointed since ancient times as the GOSPEL CANTICLE in Evening Prayer (Vespers).

Maltese cross. See CROSS.

Mandatum. See MAUNDY.

Maniple (MAN-i-pul; Middle English from Old French, handful, from Latin *manipulus*, a handful). A cloth, usually in the proper liturgical color, worn on the left forearm of the presiding minister and the deacon at the Eucharist. It is a vestigal remnant of a hand towel used to wipe the sweat from the brow of ministers and communicants and to dry the hands, and later to cleanse the rim of the chalice. The traditional prayer while vesting associates the maniple with the tears and sorrow of this world, recalling the punishment of Adam; "by the sweat of your face you shall eat bread until you return to the ground" ("May I be worthy, Lord, to bear the hard lot of tears and sorrow that with joy I may receive the reward of my labor"). The use of the maniple has been optional in the Roman Catholic church since 1967; it is not mentioned in the missal of 1969.

Manual acts (Middle English from Latin *manualis*, of the hand). The actions of the presiding minister in connection with the words of institution, taking and lifting the bread, taking and lifting the chalice, lifting the bread and cup at the doxology at the conclusion of the GREAT THANKSGIVING.

Mark. See EVANGELISTS' SYMBOLS.

Martyrology (MAR-ter-OLL-gee; Greek *logos*, word, account). A book containing the names of saints and martyrs whose days are to be observed, with the dates of their commemoration.

Martyrs (MAR-ters; Old English from Greek *martus*, witness). Those holy men and women who have followed Christ so closely that they, like him, gave their lives for the faith. The martyrs were the first saints to be commemorated on the Christian calendar.

Mary. Three feasts honor the blessed Virgin Mary: her IMMACULATE CONCEPTION (December 8), originating in the East ca. 700; her NATIVITY (September 8), originating in the East ca. 500; and her ASSUMPTION (August 15), called in the East the Dormition, her "Falling Asleep," originating in the East in the mid-fifth century. Three feasts honor her as the mother of Christ: the ANNUNCIATION (March 25), originating in the East in the fifth century; the VISITATION (May 31), a Western feast introduced in 1263; and the PRESENTATION (February 2), originating in the East in the fourth century. The present Roman calendar has recovered an ancient feast on January 1 now called the Solemnity of Mary the Mother of God, and it provides other memorials of Mary: Our Lady of Lourdes (February 11), the Immaculate Heart of Mary (Saturday after the Sacred Heart of Jesus), Our Lady of Mount Carmel (July 16), the Queenship of Mary (August 22), Our Lady of Sorrows (September 15), Our Lady of the Rosary (October 7), the PRESENTATION OF MARY (November 21). Other local feasts are observed in individual churches; also, May is dedicated to Mary (originating in the seventeenth century), and October is rosary month (originating in the late nineteenth century). In the Byzantine, West Syrian, and East Syrian rites, December 26 is a feast of Mary; January 16 is a feast of Mary in the Coptic church.

Mass (Old English from Latin *missa*, probably from the dismissal at the end of the Roman rite, *Ite, missa est*, Go, it is the dismissal). The central service of the Christian church, the Holy Communion, the Eucharist. Luther retained the name, and many Lutheran churches around the world still use the name, as do many Anglican churches.

Mass of the catechumens (*missa catechumenorum*). The first part of the mass, the liturgy of the word, after which anciently the CATECHUMENS were dismissed with a blessing.

Mass of the faithful (*missa fidelium*). The second half of the mass, the liturgy of the Sacrament, the holy mysteries, to which anciently only the baptized were admitted; catechumens, penitents, and those under discipline were excluded.

Mass, names of the. Many names have been given to the central action of Christianity through history: the Breaking of Bread (1 Corinthians 10:16; Acts 2:42), the Lord's Supper (1 Corinthians 11:20), the Eucharist (*Didache* 9.5), the Divine Liturgy (the common name in the Eastern churches), the Offering (*oblatio*, used by Etheria and the Armenians), the Sacrifice (*sacrificium*, used by Tertullian and Cyprian), Prosphora (a term used occasionally in the Greek East), ANAPHORA, Kurbono or Kurbana (gift, used in East and West Syria), Korobho (approach [to, of God], in West Syria), the Holy (*sacrum*), Dominicum (the Lord's, in North Africa and Rome in the third and fourth centuries), the Service (*Amt*, in German), the Action (*actio*), Agenda (the order).

Master of ceremonies. See CAEREMONIARIUS.

Matins (MAT-ins; Middle English from Latin [*vigiliae*] *matutinae*, [vigils, watches] of the morning). 1. The first of the traditional hours of prayer in the daily office, prayed originally at midnight (NOCTURNS said during the hours of darkness) but often combined with LAUDS and prayed at daybreak both for convenience and, after the introduction of PRIME at the beginning of the day's work, for the preservation of the pattern of the psalmist "seven times a day I praise you" (Psalm 119:164). See LITURGY OF THE HOURS. 2. Morning Prayer in Lutheran and Anglican churches, which combines elements of the traditional Matins (in England spelled Mattins), Lauds, and Prime. The name is used without an article: Matins, not "a Matins."

Matthew. See APOSTLES' SYMBOLS; see EVANGELISTS' SYMBOLS.

Matthias. See APOSTLES' SYMBOLS.

Maundy (MAWN-dee). An English term for the washing of the feet on Thursday in Holy Week, called **Maundy Thursday**, derived from the Latin *mandatum*, commandment; on this day Jesus said to his disciples, "I give you a new commandment, that you love one another" (John 13:34).

Media vita in morte sumus (MAY-dee-a VEE-ta in MORE-tay SOO-moose; Latin, In the midst of life we are in death). An antiphon first found in eleventh-century manuscripts, attributed erroneously to Notker Balbulus (d. 910), used as an antiphon to the NUNC DIMITTIS at Compline during the middle of Lent. The antiphon was popular in Germany; Luther made a hymn translation of it, *Mitten wir im Leben sind*, "Even as we live each day."

Memento Domini (me-MEN-toe; Latin, Remember, Lord). The

second section and part of the earlier stratum of the Roman CANON in which the celebrant prays for the church militant.

Memento etiam (ET-ee-ahm; Latin, Remember also). The tenth section of the Roman CANON, a later addition to the earlier stratum, in which the celebrant prays that those who have died with the sign of faith be given a place of refreshment, light, and peace.

Memorial (Middle English from Latin *memoria*, memory). In current Roman Catholic use, a holy day (*memoria*) ranking below a FEAST, on which neither GLORIA IN EXCELSIS nor creed is said. **Optional memorials** are lesser observances, not required but which may be celebrated if desired.

Memorial collects. Prayers that followed the collect for the day in the medieval rites, by which lesser observances that fell on the same day were remembered.

Menorah (men-OR-ah; Hebrew, candlestick). 1. A seven-branched candelabrum of the Jewish Temple, symbolizing the seven days of creation (Exodus 37:17-24). 2. A nine-branched candelabrum used in the celebration of Hannukah, the eight-day festival commemorating the rededication of the Temple by Judas Maccabaeus in 165 B.C.E.

Mensa (Latin, table). The top surface of an altar.

Metrical psalter. A version of the Hebrew Psalms in metrical En-

glish verse so that they may be sung to hymn tunes. Such psalters are an important stage in the development of hymnody following the Reformation. Notable metrical psalters include Sternhold and Hopkins, *The Whole Book of Psalms* (1556, 1562); Henry Ainsworth, *Booke of Psalms*, published for the English Puritans in Holland in 1612 and brought to America by the Pilgrims; the *Bay Psalm Book*, published in Cambridge, Massachusetts, in 1640; Nahum Tate and Nicholas Brady, *A New Version of the Psalms of David* (1696), which made Sternhold and Hopkins the "Old Version."

Metropolitan (Middle English from Greek *metropolites*, a citizen of a metropolis). The PRIMATE of an ecclesiastical PROVINCE. 1. In the Western church, an archbishop who has authority over bishops. 2. In the Eastern Orthodox church, a bishop ranking next below the PATRIARCH, who serves as the head of a PROVINCE.

Michael. See ANGELS.

Mid-Lent. Laetare, Refreshment Sunday, the fourth Sunday in Lent, marked by a lessening of the Lenten discipline as an encouragement to maintain the rigors of the season until Easter.

Milk and honey. As reported in the APOSTOLIC TRADITION, given to the newly baptized at their baptismal Eucharist, recalling Joshua 5:6, signifying that in the fullness of Christianity is found the fulfillment of the promise of a land, the New Canaan. The baptized drank three times each of three chalices: one with water to signify washing and cleansing (see John 7:38), a second with milk and honey, and a third with the consecrated wine.

Minister (Middle English from Latin *minister*, servant). The person who performs a particular service of the church. The presiding minister at the Eucharist must be ordained, assisting ministers need not be, indeed should not all be ordained, so as to involve laypeople in the leadership of the service.

Ministerial acts. An older name for the collection of services and orders now called OCCASIONAL SERVICES.

Minster (Old English from Latin *monasterium*, monastery). A British term for a monastery church or for certain large churches or cathedrals.

Misereatur (me-se-ray-AH-toor; Latin, May [Almighty God] have mercy [upon you]). The absolution given at the beginning of the medieval Roman mass, "May Almighty God have mercy on you, forgive you your sins, and bring you to eternal life."

Misericordia Domini (Miss-er-a-CORD-ee-a DOM-in-ee; Latin, The mercies of the Lord). The name given to the second Sunday after Easter in medieval missals and in Lutheran use, from the first word of the INTROIT, "[The earth is full of] the goodness of the Lord." In the *Common Service Book* the Latin plural was inexplicably given an English plural form: *Misericordias Domini*.

Missa catechumenorum. See MASS OF THE CATECHUMENS.

Missa fidelium. See MASS OF THE FAITHFUL.

Missa sicca. See DRY MASS.

Missal (Latin *missa*, mass). The altar book containing the services of the church for the use of those who minister at the altar. A book containing all the texts of the mass, including the choir anthems and lessons, that in the Middle Ages replaced the earlier SACRAMENTARY.

Missal stand. A low desk of wood or metal or a cushion to hold the altar book, freeing the minister's hands for liturgical gestures and the MANUAL ACTS. Properly, the missal stand is on the MENSA only during service time when it is needed; otherwise, it is kept on a CREDENCE table or shelf.

Missale Francorum (miss-AL-ee fran-KO-rum; Latin, Frankish missal). An incomplete sacra-mentary, closely related to the GELASIAN sacramentary, containing rites of ordination, blessing of widows and virgins, consecration of altars, and eleven masses. The manuscript was written in France ca. 700, although some connect it with the Gelasian sacramentary.

Missale Gallicanus vetus (gal-i-KAN-us VAY-tus; Latin, old Gallican missal). Fragments of two Gallican sacramentaries written in the eighth century. The first contains a mass for the feast of St. Germanus, forms for the consecration of widows and virgins, a mass and sermon for use in handing over the creed to catechumens; the second contains masses for Advent, Lent, Easter, and the ROGATION DAYS.

Missale Gothicum (GOTH-i-cum; Latin, Gothic missal). A Gallican sacramentary written ca. 700, probably drawn up for the church at Atun. It contains masses for Christmas Eve through Pentecost with certain saints' days interspersed. The name Missale Gothicum, added to the manuscript in the fifteenth century, led to the mistaken belief that it came from the province of Narbonne when it was under Visigothic rule.

Missale mixtum (Latin, mixed, composite missal). A complete Mozarabic sacramentary, compiled by Cardinal Ximines from existing manuscripts and published in 1500.

Miter (MITE-er; Middle English from Greek *mitra*, a turban). The liturgical hat worn by a bishop when exercising episcopal authority. Two bands called **lappets** hang from the back down on the shoulders and maintain a vestigial relation with the original band bound about the head. The miter was first worn indoors in the eleventh century. In the Eastern church, the miter takes the form of a closed crown or diadem.

Mixed chalice. The addition of a small amount of water to the wine in the chalice when it is prepared at the OFFERTORY. The practice derives from the custom in the classical world of never drinking wine unmixed with water (the wine always being added to the water, never the water to the wine because that suggested dilution); the practice was then given the symbolic interpretation of representing the blood and water that flowed from Christ's side on the cross.

Monastic office. See CATHEDRAL OFFICE.

Money bag. 1. A symbol of Matthew, the apostle and evangelist, who was a tax collector before becoming a follower of Jesus. 2. Often with thirty pieces of silver, a symbol of Judas, who betrayed Jesus for money.

Monogenes (mon-oh-GEN-ace; Greek, only begotten). A sixth-century hymn beginning "Only begotten Son and Word of God," addressed to the triumphant Redeemer, concluding the second antiphon of the ENARXIS of Eastern liturgies.

Monophysite (ma-NOFF-a-site; Greek *mono phusis*, one nature). One who holds that Christ's nature is entirely and exclusively divine, even though he took on an earthly body and human form. The Coptic and Syrian churches maintain this doctrine.

Monstrance (MON-strance; Middle English from Latin *monstrare*, to show). A ceremonial and transparent PYX for displaying the consecrated bread of the Eucharist for adoration. Also called an **ostensorium**.

Month's mind. A requiem mass celebrated on the thirtieth day after a death or burial, derived from Jewish custom (Numbers 20:29; Deuteronomy 34:8).

Morning Prayer. Now the common designation in the Anglican, Lutheran, and Roman Catholic churches of the principal office of prayer for early morning, formerly in the Roman church called LAUDS. See MATINS.

Morse (Middle English from Latin *morsus*, a catch). The ornamented clasp for fastening the front of a cope.

Motet (moe-TET; Middle English from Old French *mot*, a phrase). An unaccompanied sacred choral composition usually for liturgical services, not a setting of the texts of the ORDINARY. The text is usually biblical.

Mothering Sunday. The fourth Sunday in Lent, LAETARE, so called from the English custom of visiting one's mother on that day, inspired by the epistle for that Sunday in the medieval lectionary in use until 1969, Galatians 4:21-31, describing the heavenly Jerusalem as the mother of Christians.

Movable feast. A festival of varying date such as Easter and those feasts dependent upon it (Ascension Day, Pentecost, Trinity Sunday, Corpus Christi).

Mozarabic (moze-AR-a-bik; Spanish *mozarabe*, from Arabic *musta'rib*, a would-be Arab). The USE of that part of Spain which was under Moorish (Arab) rule after 711 until 1085; sometimes called the **Visigothic rite**, since the Visigoths occupied Spain from 470 and recognized the liturgy as the official rite in 633. The rite dates from perhaps 400 and is preserved in the practice of a chapel in the cathedral of Toledo.

Mozetta or **mozzetta** (moe-ZET-ta; Italian, short for *almozetta*, little cape, from Latin *almutia*; see ALMUCE). An elbow-length cape with a small hood attached to the back of the neck. It buttons down the front and is a Latinate version of the ancient form of the doctor's hood.

Mundatory (MUN-da-tory; Latin *mundare*, to cleanse). A PURIFICATOR.

Mystagogia (mist-a-GO-gee-a; Greek *mustagogos*, leader of initiates). Instruction in the mysteries, that is, the teachings of Christianity, as a continuation of the instruction given before baptism and part of the initiation into the Christian faith and life.

Mysteries. An ancient name for the Eucharist. Christians under persecution from shortly after Justin's death until the death of Constantine were under suspicion and sporadic persecution and so kept their services secret, revealing them only to the initiate.

Mysterium (Latin, mystery). The Institution Narrative in the eucharistic prayer, so called because in such rites as the Spanish and French this section of the prayer was said silently by the priest.

Nn

Names, recitation of the. The reading of the names of those on whose behalf a particular Eucharist is being celebrated. In France and Spain this naming was attached to the offering; in Rome, Milan, and Egypt it is inserted into the eucharistic prayer.

Narrenfest. See FEAST OF FOOLS.

Narthex (Greek, an enclosure). The vestibule or entryway of a church; originally a deep porch at the entrance of a church.

Natale or **Natalita** (na-TAHL-ay, na-TAHL-ee-ta; Latin, birthday). The day of a martyr's birth into eternal life, dying in this world to be born into heaven. Later the term was used for the anniversary of any saint.

Natalis calicis (na-TAHL-ees KAHL-i-keese; Latin, [day of] the birthday of the chalice). A name for MAUNDY Thursday in certain medieval missals.

Nativity of Christ. The celebration of the birth of Christ begins with Evening Prayer on December 24 and continues through the octave of Christmas, January 1, until the EPIPHANY.

Nativity of John the Baptist. The birth of John is celebrated on June 24, six months before the birth of Jesus, according to the chronology of Luke 1:26, 36. The feast dates from the fourth century; the commemoration was retained on Lutheran and Anglican calendars after the Reformation.

Nativity of Mary. The birth of the mother of our Lord is celebrated on September 8, nine months after the celebration of her Immaculate Conception, December 8. The feast dates from the fifth century in the East and was celebrated in Rome by the seventh century. It was retained on several Lutheran calendars after the Reformation.

Nave (NAY-v; Latin *navis*, ship; Greek *naos*, ship, the principal area of a temple). The principal portion of a church, between the NARTHEX and the CHOIR or CROSSING. The word, derived from "ship" in Latin and Greek, is explained as relating to the church as the ark of salvation, or more likely to the shiplike appearance of the nave.

Navicula (na-VIK-you-la; Latin, boat). The boat for carrying incense for replenishing the CENSER.

Neophyte (NEE-oh-fite; Greek, newly planted, newly born, possessing a new nature). The ancient liturgical name for the newly baptized.

New fire, blessing of. See BLESSING OF THE NEW FIRE.

Nicene Creed (nye-SEEN). The creed traditionally associated with the Eucharist, begun in the East, amplified at the Council of Nicaea in 325 from whence it receives its name, expanded at Constantinople in 381, and adopted at Chalcedon in 451. The creed entered the Eucharist during the christological controversies of the fifth century in the East; by the end of the sixth century the practice had spread to the West. The FILIOQUE was added by the Third Council of Toledo in 589.

Nimbus (Latin, cloud). Any of several devices of Christian iconography symbolizing sanctity, usually a radiance or circle above or behind the heads of saints and God. Also called a HALO. A square nimbus indicates that the person was living at the time the representation was made.

Nobis quoque (NO-bis KWO-kway; Latin, to us also). The eleventh section of the Roman CANON, a later addition to the earlier strata, beginning "To us sinners, your servants, also grant some part . . . with all your saints. . . ."

Nocturn (NOCK-turn; Middle English from Latin *nocturnus*, at night). One of the three divisions of MATINS, the nocturnal (night) office of the Liturgy of the Hours.

None or **Nones** (KNOWN; Latin *nona*, the ninth hour). Prayer in mid-afternoon, the ninth hour (af-ter sunrise) of the Roman day, about 3 p.m. One of the LITTLE HOURS of the daily prayer of the church.

Non-jurors. Members of the Church of England who, after 1688, refused to take the Oath of Allegiance and Supremacy to William and Mary because of their former oath to James II and his successors. They published their own liturgies from 1718 on, revised along Eastern lines. By the latter part of the eighteenth century they had virtually disappeared.

North. The GOSPEL SIDE of the SANCTUARY, the left side as one faces the altar from the nave. It is the side of honor, to the right of the altar when one looks toward the nave. An oddity of Anglican practice for a time after the Reformation was the requirement that the priest celebrate the Holy Communion from the north end of the altar to avoid the medieval Catholic practice of the priest facing the altar, back to the people.

Novena (no-VEE-na; Latin, nine each). Prayers and devotions said for nine successive days, particularly the nine days between Ascension Day and Pentecost during which the church prays earnestly for the outpouring of the Holy Spirit.

Number symbolism. Certain numbers are used in ecclesiastical architecture, furnishing, decoration, liturgy, and liturgical action with symbolic importance: **one**, the unity of God; **two**, the two natures of Christ, divine and human, or the two Testaments, Old and New; **three**, the Holy Trinity; **four**, the four evangelists, the four Gospels, the four directions of the compass; **five**, the five wounds of Christ in hands and feet and side, Christ and the evangelists; **six**, the days of creation, sin (being one less than seven); **seven**, the holy number of completeness and perfection, the days of the week, the gifts of the Holy Spirit (see under STAR), the seven virtues (faith, hope, charity; justice, prudence, fortitude, temperance), the lamps before the throne of God (Revelation 4:5), the seven sacraments of the Catholic tradition; **eight**, the new creation, the eighth day, regeneration; **nine**, three times three, triply holy; **ten**, the ten commandments; **twelve**, the twelve tribes of Israel, the twelve apostles.

Nunc Dimittis (nunc di-MIT-iss; Latin, now dismiss). The song of Simeon from Luke 2:29-32, beginning "Lord, now you let your servant go in peace," appointed since ancient times as the GOSPEL CANTICLE at COMPLINE; in Lutheran use it is frequently the post-communion canticle.

Oo

O Antiphons. The seven splendid "greater antiphons," of unknown authorship, in use by the eighth century, used with the MAGNIFICAT at Vespers from December 17 through December 23. Each is similar in structure to a collect and begins with an invocation of the Messiah under an Old Testament title, continues with an amplification giving an attribute of the Messiah and developing the invocation, and concludes with a fervent appeal that makes reference to the invocation. The antiphons begin: O Sapientia (Wisdom), O Adonai, O Radix Jesse (Root of Jesse), O Clavis David (Key of David), O Oriens (Dayspring), O Rex Gentium (King of the nations), O Emmanuel. To these seven the Sarum, York, and Hereford breviaries add an eighth to the Virgin Mary, "O Virgo virginum" (O virgin of virgins); the Sarum breviary also added a ninth, to St. Thomas, "O Thoma didyme" (O Thomas didymus).

O Sapientia (sap-ee-EN-si-a; Latin, O wisdom). The first of the O ANTIPHONS, hence December 17 was on many ancient calendars called O Sapientia to indicate the beginning of the use of the greater antiphons, marking the beginning of the second part of Advent, one week before Christmas Eve.

Oblation (ob-LAY-shun; Middle English from Latin *oblatio*, an offering). 1. The name in the early church for the Eucharist. 2. The offerings of bread and wine. 3. The offering of the Christian's life and abilities to the service of God.

Obsecration (ob-se-CRAY-shun; Latin *obsecrare*, to ask on sacred grounds). A fervent petition, calling upon God to grant a request. Specifically the section of the Litany in which the petitions are introduced with the word "by" ("by the mystery of your incarnation; by your holy birth . . . Help us good Lord"), pleading for mercy on the ground of Christ's redemptive acts.

Occasional services. Services designed for specific occasions such as the dedication of a church, as opposed to the more general services of Holy Communion and daily prayer, which are used regularly and are appropriate for a variety of occasions.

Occurrence (Latin *occurrere*, to run to meet). Two festivals falling on the same day. The greater festival takes PRECEDENCE and prevails,

89

the lesser festival being postponed until the next open date. See CONCURRENCE.

Octave (Latin *octavus*, eighth). 1. The eighth day of a festival, an echo of the feast one week later. 2. The weeklong celebration of a festival, prolonging the joy over eight days and making a liturgical week of feasts. Although in the Middle Ages octaves abounded, only Easter and Christmas have octaves in the present calendars of the Western church. See GREAT OCTAVE.

Oculi (OH-koo-lee; Latin, eyes). The name of the third Sunday in Lent in medieval missals and in Lutheran use, from the first words of the INTROIT for the day, "My eyes are ever toward the Lord."

Offering (Latin *offere*, to carry up, offer). 1. The presentation of oneself for the service of God as commanded in Romans 12:1. 2. The presentation of the gifts of bread and wine for the service of God, returning to the Creator the gifts of wheat and grapes as human hands and skill have transformed them, offering them for further transformation, revaluation, and revelation as vehicles of grace in the Eucharist. 3. The ANAPHORA. 4. The Eucharist. 5. In Protestant churches, the gathering and presentation of gifts of money for the support of the church.

Offertory (Latin *offerre*, to carry up, offer). 1. Verses from the psalms or other sources sung while the offering is presented or while the ELEMENTS are prepared for the Holy Communion. 2. The action of bringing up the (alms and) OBLATIONS and their presentation at the altar.

Offertory veil. 1. Originally a cloth in which the offerings were received from the people, the veil became a cover for the offerings brought by the people for presentation at the altar. 2. In Anglican use, a long silk cloth worn over the shoulders of a clerk or subdeacon, muffling the hands while taking the sacramental vessels to the altar at the offertory and from the altar after the Eucharist to prevent tarnishing the vessels. See SUDARY.

Office (Latin *officium*, a duty, obligation, service). 1. The cycle of daily prayer including Morning Prayer, Evening Prayer, and Compline, called the DIVINE OFFICE or the CHOIR OFFICE or the LITURGY OF THE HOURS or the CANONICAL HOURS. 2. A specially constructed form of worship for a specific occasion, usually less elaborate than an ORDER and not in itself a complete service.

Office Hymn. A hymn appointed for use in the daily office; the practice is first mentioned in the Rule of St. Benedict. The office hymns at Vespers have traditionally dealt with the work of creation on the successive days of the week, following the pattern of Genesis 1, "There was evening and there was morning, the first day."

Office lights. See LIGHTS.

Office of Readings. In the Liturgy of the Hours, the office derived from MATINS; may be prayed at any hour of the day, giving an extensive meditation on Scripture and the writings of spiritual authors.

Oil. In the ancient world a medicine for healing, a source of light (in lamps), and thus of joy. Oil from the olive tree came to suggest reconciliation and peace (the dove brought Noah an olive leaf as the flood waters receded). Christianity distinguishes three kinds of oil: **oil of catechumens**, used in anointing those who are preparing for Holy Baptism; **oil of the sick**, used to anoint those who are seriously ill; and CHRISM (oil to which a fragrance has been added), used in the anointing in Holy Baptism to show the seal of the Spirit.

Omega. See ALPHA AND OMEGA.

Omophorion (Greek, maintaining the same [faith]). A STOLE, similar to the ORARION, worn by bishops of the BYZANTINE RITE over their SAKKOS; in some ways it corresponds to the Latin PALLIUM.

Orale (oh-RALL-ay). The name used in the time of Innocent III for the FANON worn by the pope.

Orans (OH-ranns; Latin, praying). The ancient posture for prayer: standing with arms outstretched and uplifted, palms upward, lifting the body and spirit upward to God and welcoming God's gifts as they descend.

Orarion (oh-RAHR-ee-on; medieval Greek from Latin *orarium*, a small towel, napkin, serviette). The Eastern deacon's STOLE, worn over the left shoulder and hanging straight down in front and back; sometimes it is passed under the right arm and again over the left shoulder before being hung down in front.

Oratory (OR-a-tory; Middle English from Latin *orare*, to pray). A small chapel designed for private prayer rather than for the public celebration of the sacraments.

Orb (Old French from Latin *orbis*, an orb, disk). A jeweled globe surmounted with a cross, part of the regalia of a sovereign. It shows the triumph of Christianity over the world.

Order (Middle English from Latin *ordo*, order, originally a row of threads on a loom). A specially constructed form of worship appropriate to a particular occasion, more elaborate than an OFFICE, being a complete service in itself.

Ordinal (OR-din-al; Latin *ordo*, order). 1. A book containing the service of ordination. 2. A book containing those occasional services requiring the leadership of a bishop.

Ordinand (Latin *ordinandus*, gerundive of *ordinare*, to ordain). A candidate for ORDINATION.

Ordinary (Latin *ordo*, order). 1. One of the invariable liturgical texts of a service, especially the Eucharist. 2. The components of a musical mass: KYRIE, GLORIA IN EXCELSIS, NICENE CREED, SANCTUS, AGNUS DEI. 3. The bishop of a diocese.

Ordination (Latin *ordo*, order). The ritual by which a person is admitted to the ministry of the church. The term is used of the ordering of deacons, of presbyters-pastors-priests-ministers, and of bishops, although the ordination of bishops is also called consecration.

Ordines Romani (OR-din-es; Latin, Roman orders). The ancient collections of ceremonial directions for the performance of the Roman rite. These church orders of the eighth to the tenth centuries are now organized thus: I-X, the mass; XI, baptism; XII-XIV, daily prayer; XV-XIX, monastic orders and rituals for the church year; XX-XXXIII, feasts of the year, especially Holy Week; XXXIV-XL, ordinations; XLI-XLIV, dedication of churches; XLV-XLVIII, the coronation of the emperor; XLIX, funerals; L, the ordo from the tenth century Romano-Germanic PONTIFICAL.

Organ (Middle English from Greek *organon*, an implement, instrument). A musical instrument in use in Christian worship since the early eighth century, consisting of a keyboard and a number of pipes supplied with wind by means of a bellows, making its sound by setting a column of air in motion. The organ has been said to be the most appropriate instrument for use in the services of the church because it alone of all instruments is able to prolong its sound indefinitely and so in an emblem of eternity, not bound by the limitations of time or the human body. Electronic pipeless instruments that contradict the very principle of the organ were introduced about 1930.

Orientate. A mid-nineteenth century liturgical variation of the existing verb "orient": to face or turn to the EAST.

Orientation (Latin *oriens*, the rising sun, east). 1. The Christian practice, traceable from the second century, of facing east for prayer, deriving from the Jewish practice of prayer offered toward the Temple in Jerusalem as the primary place of the presence of God. 2. The practice of locating churches so that the altar is toward the EAST, the direction of the rising sun and symbolic of the expectation of the second coming (Matthew 24:27). 3. The practice used with an altar in the eastward position (against or close to the wall) of the minister facing the altar for all parts of the service which are not directly addressed to the congregation. The practice was encouraged by the first of the general rubrics in the *Common Service Book* and the *Service Book and Hymnal*.

Orientes partibus (or-ee-EN-tays PAR-ti-buse; Latin, from Eastern regions). A hymn tune composed by Pierre de Corbeil ca. 1200. See Ass, FEAST OF THE.

Ornaments rubric. A controverted rubric inserted in the 1559 *Book of Common Prayer* declaring that the ornaments of the church and its ministers were to be those authorized by parliament in the second year of the reign of Edward VI.

Orphrey (OR-free; Middle English from Latin *aurum*, gold). A band of elaborate embroidery used to decorate ecclesiastical VESTMENTS and PARAMENTS.

Orthros (ORTH-rahs; Greek, dawn). The morning office celebrated in the Eastern church, corresponding to Matins in the Western office.

Osculatorium (os-koo-la-TOR-ee-um). See PAX BOARD.

Ostensorium (os-ten-SOAR-ee-um; Latin *ostendere*, to show). See MONSTRANCE.

Ostiarius (os-tee-ARE-ee-us; Latin, a doorkeeper). The first of the seven medieval orders of ministry.

Our Father. The Lord's Prayer, used three times each day, according to the *DIDACHE*; used at the conclusion of the GREAT THANKSGIVING as the table prayer of the people of God before communion; used as the conclusion of the prayers in Morning and Evening Prayer in Roman and Lutheran use, as the beginning of the prayers in the OFFICE in Anglican use, and at other times.

Pain benit (PAN ben-EE; French, blessed bread). Bread formerly given to the people after mass in French and Canadian churches. See ANTIDORON.

Palitza. A diamond-shaped piece of brocade suspended by one corner on the right hip of a priest of the Byzantine rite, conferred as a reward of honor. See EPIGONATION.

Pall (Old English from Latin *pallium*, a cover, cloak). 1. The **eucharistic pall** is a stiffened piece of cloth used to cover the chalice during the Holy Communion, except during the VERBA or the entire EUCHARISTIC PRAYER and the distribution of communion, to keep foreign objects from falling into it. 2. The **funeral pall** is a large cloth used to cover the coffin during the Burial of the Dead, recalling the baptismal garment and the robe of righteousness (Matthew 22:11-12; Galatians 3:27), and in modern practice is usually white to suggest Easter and the resurrection. Earlier custom prescribed violet or black to represent mourning.

Pallium (PAL-ee-um; Latin, a cloak, cover). A circular band of white wool with a strip hanging down in the front and the back, marked with six purple crosses, worn over the CHASUBLE by the pope and conferred by him on archbishops and sometimes on bishops, deriving from an article of Roman dress.

Palm (Middle English *palme* from Latin *palma*, palm [of the hand], hence, from the resemblance of the leaves to the outspread human hand, the palm tree). A sign of victory (Psalm 92:12; Matthew 21:1-9), especially the victory of martyrs (Revelation 7:9-10).

Palm Sunday. See PASSION SUNDAY.

Palmarum (palm-ARE-um; Latin [day] of the palms). The title in medieval missals and in Lutheran service books for the sixth Sunday in Lent, now called the Sunday of the Passion.

Palmesel (palm AY-sel; German, palm donkey). A wooden figure of Christ seated on a donkey, brought into churches in Germany on Palm Sunday (the Sunday of the Passion) in the Middle Ages, accompanied by hymns, to dramatize and make visual the processional Gospel for the day, telling of the triumphal entry.

Panagia. See PECTORAL CROSS.

Pange, lingua, gloriosi corporis mysterium (Latin, Sing [my] tongue, of the mystery of the

94

glorious body). A Latin hymn written in 1263 by Thomas Aquinas for the then-new office of CORPUS CHRISTI. It is known in several English translations, among them John Mason Neale's "Of the glorious body telling." See TANTUM ERGO.

Pange, lingua, gloriosi proelium certaminis. A Latin hymn of ten unrhymed trochaic tetrameter stanzas by Venantius Fortunatus (530-609), extensively used in the liturgy of HOLY WEEK and on feasts of the HOLY CROSS. It is known in English in John Mason Neale's translation, "Sing, my tongue, the glorious battle."

Paraclete (PAR-a-cleat; Greek, helper, intercessor). The Holy Spirit (John 14:26).

Paraments (PAR-a-ments; Latin *parare*, to prepare). A general name for the cloths in the various liturgical colors used on the altar, pulpit, and lectern.

Parasceve (PAR-ah-skayve; from Greek *paraskeve*, preparation). A name for Good Friday in certain medieval missals. The name derives from the Jewish designation of Friday as the preparation for the Sabbath (see Matthew 27:62; Mark 15:42; Luke 13:54; John 19:31, 42).

Pasch(a) (PAS-ka; Greek *paska* from Hebrew *pesa(c)h*, the Passover). The celebration of the passion, death, and resurrection of Christ during the TRIDUUM, Maundy Thursday evening through the dawn of Easter. The Greek word *paska* applies both to the Jewish Passover and to the Christian Easter.

Pascha annotinum (an-OH-tee-num; Latin, one year old Pasch). A commemoration of the anniversary of a baptism with thanksgiving and prayer. The custom originated in the seventh century as the Easter Vigil, with its renewal of baptismal vows, disappeared and baptism became privatized.

Paschal (PASS-kel; Middle English from Greek *paska*). Having to do with the Pasch or Easter.

Paschal Blessing. A commemoration of the resurrection of Christ, used in the *Lutheran Book of Worship* to conclude Morning Prayer on Sundays. The office has its origin in the church in Jerusalem, as reported by Egeria in the fourth century, and consists of the singing of a resurrection Gospel (Luke 24:1-7), the TE DEUM, a collect, and a blessing.

Paschal candle. A massive candle, blessed and invested with symbolic importance at the Easter Vigil, used during Easter to show the presence of the risen Christ among his people; it is therefore also used at baptisms and funerals as a sign of dying and rising with Christ. During Easter its place is near the GOSPEL SIDE of the altar; outside of Easter its place is often near the baptismal font.

Passing Bell. See BELL, PASSING.

Passion History. See HISTORY OF THE PASSION.

Passion Sunday. 1. Until 1969, the fifth Sunday in Lent and the beginning of **Passion Week**, the week before HOLY WEEK. 2. After the calendar reforms of the later twentieth century, the sixth Sunday in Lent, properly called the Sunday of the Passion, popularly still called Palm Sunday.

Passion symbols. Among the symbols of the suffering and death of Christ are these: a basin and ewer, recalling Pilate's washing his hands of responsibility for Jesus' death; the COCK; the CROWN of thorns; a LADDER; nails, usually three (one for each hand and one through both feet together) used to fasten the body of Jesus to the cross; scourges, leather whips with which Jesus was beaten.

Passiontide. The fortnight between PASSION SUNDAY (the fifth Sunday in Lent) and Easter. With the calendar reforms, beginning in 1969, the term is now obsolete.

Passover (pass over, a translation of Hebrew *pesa(c)h*, a passing over). The eight-day Jewish commemoration, beginning on the 14th of Nisan, of the deliverance from slavery in Egypt, the passage through the Red Sea, and the entrance into freedom.

Pastoral staff. See CROZIER.

Paten (PATT-en; Middle English; Latin *patina*, a dish). A plate, usually made of gold or silver lined with gold, used to hold the bread of the Holy Communion when the bread is in the form of HOSTS (wafers). In Western use it is usually constructed with a depression in the center, large enough to fit into the top of the chalice, the design of which it usually matches, for convenient carrying to and from the altar. In Eastern use the paten, called a DISKOS, is usually set on a stem or base.

Patriarch (Middle English from Greek *pater*, father). 1. A title, dating from the sixth century, for the bishops of Constantinople, Alexandria, Antioch, Jerusalem, or Rome with authority over other bishops and, later, for the Orthodox bishops of Moscow, Serbia, or Rumania. 2. The head of the Coptic, Armenian, Syrian Jacobite, or Nestorian churches.

Patronal festival. The annual celebration of the feast day of the saint for whom a church is named.

Paul. See APOSTLES' SYMBOLS.

Pax (POX; Latin, peace). 1. The PEACE given and received at the Eucharist. 2. The salutation "The peace of the Lord be with you always" that precedes the offering in the Lutheran and Episcopal liturgy of Holy Communion or, in the Roman rite (and optionally in the Lutheran rite), precedes the distribution of communion.

Pax board. A board bearing the image of the crucifixion or of another biblical scene or saint passed among the communicants at the

PEACE for each to kiss. It is therefore also called an **osculatorium** (Latin *osculari*, to kiss).

Peace. See KISS OF PEACE.

Peacock (Old English *pea*, peafowl). A symbol of resurrection, because each year it sheds its feathers and grows new and more brilliant ones; moreover, according to legend, the flesh of the peacock is incorruptible.

Peal (Middle English *pele*, a summons to church by a bell, from *appelen*, to appeal). A ringing of from three to eight bells musically tuned to each other. The only melodies regarded as appropriate to a peal are the complicated permutations known as "changes," brought to perfection in English churches. Hymn tunes are appropriate only to CARILLONS.

Pectoral cross (PECK-ter-al; Latin *pectora*, breast). A ceremonial cross worn on the breast. Since the latter part of the seventeenth century the pectoral cross has been common to bishops. In the Eastern churches the bishop wears a **panagia**, a circular or oval icon, instead of a cross.

Pelican (Old English from Greek *pelekus*, an ax, probably from the shape of its bill). A symbol of Christ's sacrifice, because legend holds that a pelican pecks open its own breast to feed its young with its blood, dying so that her young may live.

Penitential psalms. The seven psalms of repentance: Psalms 6, 32, 38, 51, 102, 130, 143.

Penitents, reconciliation of. See RECONCILIATION OF PENITENTS.

Pennon (PEN-en; Middle English from Latin *penna*, a wing). A long, narrow flag ending in two points, borne upon a lance. See AGNUS DEI.

Pentecost (PEN-ta-cost; Old English from Greek *pentakoste*, the fiftieth day). 1. The fiftieth day after Easter, WHITSUNDAY. 2. More anciently, the fifty days of Easter. Pentecost is the culmination of Easter, not a season of the church year.

Per quem (PEAR KWEM; Latin, through whom). The final section and part of the earlier stratum of the Roman CANON, "through whom, Lord, you always create, sanctify, enliven, bless, and give us these good things," leading into the concluding doxology.

Pericope (per-IK-oh-pee; Greek, a section). A portion of the Bible appointed to be read in the services of the church.

Peter. See APOSTLES' SYMBOLS.

Petitions (Middle English from Latin *petere*, to seek, ask). A section of supplications and intercessions in the Litany: "To rule and govern your holy catholic Church . . . we implore you to hear us, good Lord."

Pew (Middle English from Old French *piue*, a raised seat, from Greek *podion*, a small base or foot). Anciently an enclosure containing chairs and kneelers built for the principal family of a parish. In the seventeenth century the term came to be used for any bench for two or more people that did not have separations between the seats.

Phelonion (fell-AHN-ee-on; Greek, a cloak). The CHASUBLE worn in the BYZANTINE RITE; a long, ample, sleeveless garment, short in the front, with an opening for the head.

Philip. See APOSTLES' SYMBOLS.

Phoenix (Middle English from Greek). A symbol of the resurrection, because the legendary bird, the only one of its kind, lived five hundred (or a thousand) years and then set fire to its nest, was consumed, and rose from the ashes to live another term.

Phos hilaron (FOSE HILL-a-ron; Greek, joyous light). A most ancient and beloved song of the church, originally sung in Greek at the lighting of the lamps at the time of Evening Prayer. This hymn to Christ, who is light from light, reflecting the glory of the immortal Father, is sung at the beginning of the LUCERNARIUM at the beginning of Evening Prayer (Vespers) in the *Lutheran Book of Worship* and in the order for Daily Evening Prayer in the *Book of Common Prayer*.

Piscina (pi-SEE-na; Latin, fish tank). A drain built into the church wall or sacristy connecting with the earth rather than a sewer, used for disposing of the baptismal water and, if it is not consumed, wine remaining in the chalice after the Holy Communion. Also called a SACRARIUM.

Plainchant or **Plainsong** (Latin *cantus planus*, unaccompanied song). Melodic, unmeasured, unaccompanied unison vocal music of the church.

Plough Monday. The Monday after the Epiphany (January 6) on which, in medieval England, ploughing was begun.

Pointing (Middle English from Latin *punctus*, pierced). An indication of how the syllables of a text are to be allotted to a chant.

Polychrome (Greek, many colored). Decorative painting in bright colors, often on wood, such as a reredos, ceiling beams, and panels.

Polyphony (pol-IF-o-nee; Greek *poluphonia*, variety of tones). Music that combines several individual voice parts into a unified whole and which emphasizes the horizontal dimension.

Pomegranite (Middle English from Old French *pome grenate*, an apple having many seeds). Shown about to burst as a symbol of Christ bursting from the tomb in resurrection. An ancient symbol of death and resurrection because it opens like a red wound, but contains within that very wound the seeds of new life. It was used to decorate the robes of Aaron (Exodus 28:33-34).

Pontifical (pon-TIFF-i-kal; Latin *pontifex*, in pre-Christian Rome a member of the highest college of priests, the title reshaped, probably from Etruscan, to suggest "bridge builder"). 1. Pertaining to a bishop, as a Pontifical Mass, a mass celebrated by a bishop. 2. A liturgical book of the Western church containing prayers and ceremonies used by a bishop; also called a **Pontificale**.

Post-communion (Latin, after communion). 1. The prayer, in the Roman rite proper to the day, said following the reception of Holy Communion and asking for a particular benefit of the Sacrament appropriate to the day or season. 2. The entire concluding section of the Eucharist, following the reception of Holy Communion through the blessing and dismissal.

Post pridie (post PREE-dee-ay; Latin, after "pridie"). The section of the eucharistic prayer following the institution narrative, so called from the opening words of the narrative *QUI PRIDIE quam pateretur*, "who the day before he suffered. . . ." Also called **post-mysterium** (after the mystery [of the consecration]) or **post-secreta** (after the secret, because the words of institution were said in a low voice).

Post Sanctus (Latin, after the Sanctus). The EUCHARISTIC PRAYER, the prayer of thanksgiving that follows the SANCTUS in the GREAT THANKSGIVING.

Postil (POSS-til; German *postille*, a book of sermons). A collection of sermons, homilies, and comments on the PERICOPES of the church year. The name derives from the customary words with which these were begun, *post illa verba scripturae*, after these words of Scripture. In the Reformation period, such collections became popular and were issued by Luther, Veit Dietrich, Johann Mathesius, Johannes Brentz, and others.

Praeconium (pry-CON-ee-um; Latin, an announcement). A liturgical announcement or solemn proclamation, specifically the **praeconium paschale**, the announcement of Easter, the EXSULTET.

Praeparatio (pry-pah-RAHT-see-oh; Latin, preparation). A name for the fourth Sunday in Advent, indicating the proximity of Christmas to which Advent points.

Prayer of the Church. The prayer of intercession which brings the liturgy of the word to a close, following the creed and preceding the Peace. It was so called in the *Service Book and Hymnal*; in the *Common Service Book* it was called the General Prayer; in the *Lutheran Book of Worship* it is simply the Prayers. In the *Book of Common Prayer* these intercessions are called the Prayers of the People.

Prayer of the Day. The name in the *Lutheran Book of Worship* for what in the Roman rite is called the Opening Prayer, and in Anglican and earlier Lutheran and Roman use is the collect. It concludes the ENTRANCE RITE and prepares for the proclamation of Scripture.

Prayer over the gifts. The name in the present Roman rite for the offertory prayer that concludes the preparation of the gifts of bread and wine before the PREFACE.

Precedence (pre-SEED-ence; Middle English from Latin *praecedere*, to go before). The priority of one commemoration over another when the two fall on the same date, as for example, when the fourth Sunday in Advent falls on December 21, St. Thomas' Day: Advent 4 takes precedence of (over) the feast of St. Thomas, which is transferred to the following day.

Precentor (pre-CEN-ter; Latin, one who sings before). The cleric responsible for directing the choral services in cathedrals.

Preces (PRAY-sees; Latin, prayers). A series of verses and responses used as prayers or used to introduce a collect or series of collects, as in Morning and Evening Prayer in the *Book of Common Prayer* and in Responsive Prayer 1 and 2 in the *Lutheran Book of Worship*.

Predella (pray-DELL-a; Italian, slab, footstool). The footpace, raised platform, or topmost step on which an altar is erected.

Preface (Latin *praefatio*, a religious form of words, a formula). The solemn proclamation of praise which begins the GREAT THANKSGIVING, from the SURSAM CORDA through the SANCTUS: "The Lord be with you . . . Lift up your hearts . . . Let us give thanks to the Lord our God . . . It is indeed right and salutary . . . Holy, holy holy. . . ."

Prefacial. Pertaining to the PREFACE; in the style of a solemn religious proclamation.

Pre-Lent. The two and one-half week "fast of the clergy" that preceded the "fast of the faithful," which began on Ash Wednesday, consisting of the Sundays of SEPTUAGESIMA, SEXAGESIMA, and QUINQUAGESIMA. A peculiarity of the Roman rite instituted late in the sixth century, this "NARTHEX to the QUADRAGESIMA" is no longer part of the Western calendar because it is thought that Lent is already long enough without a further extension.

Presanctified. The Mass of the Presanctified, a term no longer used in the Roman liturgical documents, is a form of the Eucharist without a consecration that is used in the Western church on Good Friday and in the Eastern church during Lent. A host consecrated at a previous mass is used for communion.

Presbyter (PRESS-bi-ter; Greek *presbuteros*, elder). Those ordained ministers of the church who traditionally advise, counsel, and assist the bishop in the bishop's ministry. A presbyter is commonly called a PRIEST.

Presentation (Middle English from Latin *praesentare*, to present). 1. The **Presentation of Our Lord** is the commemoration on February 2 of the presentation of the infant Jesus in the Temple by his parents in accordance with the law, and the ritual purification of his mother after childbirth, forty days after Christmas. 2. The **Presentation of Mary** is the commemoration on November 21 of the presentation of the Blessed Virgin in the Temple by her parents (traditionally identified as Anna and Joachim).

Presepio (pray-SEP-ee-o; Latin, crib, manger). The manger-crib of Christ; a group of statuary of which the central subject is the infant Christ in the manger.

Presiding minister (Latin *praesedere*, to sit in front of). The person who presides at a liturgical service, especially the Holy Communion. In the *Lutheran Book of Worship* the name is reserved to those who have been received by ordination into the ministry of word and sacrament in the church; in Roman Catholic usage the term is not always limited to the ordained. The president of the eucharistic assembly, however, must be an ordained minister (PRESBYTER), for the president represents the ministry of the whole church.

Prex (Latin, prayer). A request offered in prayer, especially as part of a longer prayer such as the Litany.

Prie-dieu (PRAY DEW; French *prier*, pray, *dieu*, God). A prayer desk which has a bench for kneeling and a support for a book or books used in private or public prayer. Sometimes called a **litany desk** from its use in Anglican churches at the entrance of the CHANCEL for praying the LITANY.

Priest (Old English from Greek *presbuteros*, an elder). A later title for the ordained minister who in the early church was called a PRESBYTER. The name is used throughout the Lutheran churches of Scandinavia and throughout the Roman, Anglican, and Orthodox churches.

Primate (PRY-mate; Middle English from Latin, *primus*, first). The ecclesiastic of highest rank in a country. The Archbishop of Uppsala is the Primate of Sweden, the Bishop of Oslo is the Primate of Norway, the Archbishop of Canterbury is the Primate of All England, the Archbishop of York is the Primate of England.

Prime (Latin *prima hora*, the first hour [of prayer]). One of the hours of daily prayer in its medieval form, said following LAUDS at the beginning of daily work (to prevent the monks from going back to bed, it has been suggested). Prime has now been suppressed in the Roman Catholic Liturgy of the Hours.

Primer (PRIM-er; Middle English from Latin *primarium*, a basic handbook). A devotional manual or book of prayers for use by the laity, giving a simplified form of the hours of prayer and other basic devotional prayers and materials.

Private confession. Making confession individually to a confessor and receiving forgiveness, differentiated from public or general confession made by a congregation.

Pro-anaphora (Greek, in front of, before the anaphora). 1. The part of the GREAT THANKSGIVING before the ANAPHORA. 2. The ANTE-COMMUNION or MASS OF THE CATECHUMENS.

Pro-cathedral (Latin *pro*, in favor of, acting as). A church used temporarily as a CATHEDRAL.

Procession of the choir. A nineteenth-century Anglican innovation almost universally adopted by all the varieties of Protestant denominations as a dramatic opening to a service of worship. It has now become the concern of Anglican and Lutheran churches to limit such processions by the choir to festive occasions and seasons.

Processional (Middle English from Latin *procedere*, to proceed). A book containing texts of litanies, hymns, and prayers prescribed for use in religious processions. During the Middle Ages such books were found in abundance.

Processional cross. Anciently, a hand cross carried in procession to the altar for use there. This was the only cross used ceremonially in the ancient church. From the medieval period onward, the processional cross is any cross on a staff of sufficient length to insure its visibility when carried at the head of a procession. Ideally, the processional cross should be placed near or behind the altar to serve as the (one) altar cross; otherwise, its significance is diminished.

Prokimenon (pro-KEEM-en-on; Greek *prokeimenon*, what is set forth). Verses from the psalms sung before the epistle in the Byzantine divine liturgy, ORTHROS, and Vespers.

Prone (French *prone*, originally a grille separating the chancel or place where notices were announced from the rest of the church). A medieval pulpit office in the vernacular language at HIGH MASS on Sundays and feasts in connection with the sermon, consisting of announcements, instruction, intercessions, and prayers.

Propers (Latin *propria*, belonging to). The variable liturgical texts of a service, which change according to the day or season of the church year, in contrast to the ORDINARY or fixed parts of the service. Older Lutheran books, such as the *Common Service Book*, used the Latin designation and spoke of "the propria."

Prose (Latin *prosus*, straightforward, direct). A liturgical composition of a rhythmic character but not in strict meter, such as "Thank the Lord and sing his praise" at the close of the Holy Communion in the *Lutheran Book of Worship*. In the medieval church, **prose** was sometimes used as a synonym for SEQUENCE.

Prostration (Middle English from Latin *prosternere*, to throw down). A penitential and dramatic intensification of the profound bow, expressing penitence, adoration, and supplication (Deuteronomy 9:18; Matthew 17:6; 26:29). It was originally part of the reverence of the altar at the beginning of mass but is now restricted to the beginning of the Good Friday liturgy, ordination, and monastic profession.

Prothesis (Greek *pro*, before, in front of, and *tithenai*, to place). 1. In the BYZANTINE RITE, a table on which the offerings of bread and wine are prepared. 2. The preparation of the elements, which takes place before the liturgy. See GREAT ENTRANCE.

Province (Middle English from Latin *provincia*, a province). A division of territory under the jurisdiction of an ARCHBISHOP or METROPOLITAN.

Psalm tones. Melodic formulas for singing the psalms. The *Lutheran Book of Worship* provides ten simple tones to which the psalms and canticles may be sung.

Psalmi idiotici (PSALM-ee id-ee-OH-ti-kee; Latin, private psalms).

Popular non-rhythmic hymns in imitation of the biblical psalms and canticles that were an important stage in the development of Christian hymnody.

Psalter (Old English from Greek *psalterion*, a song, psalm). A collection of psalms; the one hundred and fifty biblical psalms; a collection of metrical versions of the psalms to facilitate singing.

Psalter, metrical. See METRICAL PSALTER.

Pulpit (Middle English from Latin *pulpitum*, a scaffold, platform). A stand for preaching or reading, often elaborately carved and decorated. In the first Christian churches the bishop preached while sitting on the CATHEDRA or chair, denoting the bishop's authority as teacher of the community. The pulpit is traditionally placed on the liturgically NORTH side of the NAVE or CHANCEL because from the Middle Ages onward the Gospel was read from the north side of the altar. See also SOUNDING BOARD.

Purificator (PURE-i-fi-ca-ter; Middle English from Latin *purificare*, to make pure). A small linen cloth used to wipe the rim of the chalice during the administration of the Holy Communion.

Pyx (PIX; Middle English from Latin *pyxis*, a little box). A receptacle designed to hold the consecrated bread of the Holy Communion.

Quadragesima (quad-ra-GHESS-i-ma; Latin, forty). The season of Lent, forty days long.

Quadrant ore. See FORTY HOURS DEVOTION.

Quaerite dominum (KWHY-ri-tay DOME-i-num; Latin, Seek the Lord). A song of Isaiah from Isaiah 55:6-11, beginning "Seek the Lord while he may be found." It is Canticle 10 in Morning Prayer, Rite II in the *Book of Common Prayer*, borrowed as Canticle 15 in the *Lutheran Book of Worship*.

Quartodecimian (KWAR-toe-de-SIM-ee-an; Latin, fourteenther). Having to do with the practice of celebrating the PASCHA, like PASSOVER, on the 14th day of the Jewish month of Nisan, regardless of the day of the week on which it falls, rather than the following Sunday. The practice was centered in Asia Minor, and the Quartodecimians survived as a sect down to the fifth century.

Quasi modo geniti (KWA-si MOH-do GEN-i-tee; Latin, as newborns). The name of the first Sunday after Easter in medieval missals and in Lutheran use, from the first words of the INTROIT for the day, "As newborn babes [desire the sincere milk of the word]."

Quem oblationem (KWEM ob-LOT-see-own-em; Latin this oblation). The third section and part of the earlier stratum of the Roman CANON, beginning "Which oblation, O God, bless, approve, ratify, and make worthy. . . ."

Qui pridie (KWEE PREE-dee-ay; Latin, who the day before). The fourth section and part of the earlier stratum of the Roman CANON, beginning the consecration of the bread and wine, "Who the day before he suffered, took bread. . . ."

Quicunque vult (kwi-CUHN-kway; Latin, whoever desires). The proper name for the creed attributed to Athanasius, the ATHANASIAN CREED.

Quinquagesima (kwin-kwa-GHESS-i-ma; Latin, fiftieth). 1. The Sunday before Ash Wednesday, being fifty days before Easter, was understood from the sixth century until the calendar reform of 1969 as "the gateway to the Passion" (the Gospel was Luke 18:31-43, "Behold, we go up to Jerusalem"), the last of the Sundays of PRE-LENT. The name was sometimes applied to the entire pre-Lenten period. 2. In its oldest use, the name was applied to the fifty days of Easter.

104

Reconciliation (Middle English from Latin *reconciliare*, to bring together again). 1. The name recovered from the GREGORIAN SACRAMENTARY and used in recent years, especially in the Roman Catholic and Episcopal churches, as a more hopeful and positive title for what had previously been called confession or penance. 2. The restoration of the right relationship between God and humanity effected by the sacrifice of Christ.

Reconciliation of Penitents. Anciently, a part of the MAUNDY Thursday liturgy, when those who had been excluded from the fellowship of the church were welcomed back in preparation for the celebration of the sacred TRIDUUM.

Red. A liturgical color suggesting fire and blood and zeal, used on the feasts of the martyrs, on Pentecost, and certain other days on which the operation of the Holy Spirit is celebrated; a deep red or crimson is used during Holy Week.

Red-letter day. Days printed in red on the calendar; the chief festivals of the church year.

Redditio symboli (red-DIT-see-o SIM-bo-lee; Latin, giving back the symbol). The public recitation of the Apostles' Creed on Maundy Thursday by the candidates for baptism to whom the creed was taught on the previous Sunday (Sunday of the Passion).

Reformation. The celebration of the reform of the Western church inspired by Luther and begun by his posting of the Ninety-five Theses on the door of the Castle Church in Wittenberg, October 31, 1517; observed in Lutheran churches on October 31 as **Reformation Day** or on the Sunday before October 31 as **Reformation Sunday**.

Refrain (Middle English from Latin *refringere*, to break off). A recurring phrase, often sung after each verse or group of verses of a psalm or canticle. This is the distinctive form of the psalm between the lessons of the Eucharist. See RESPONSORIAL PSALMODY.

Refreshment Sunday. The fourth Sunday in Lent, LAETARE, so called from the lessening of the Lenten discipline on that Sunday. See MID-LENT.

Regina coeli (ray-GEE-na CHAY-lee; Latin, queen of heaven). One of four antiphons to the Blessed Virgin Mary sung to conclude daily prayer, found in a manuscript of 1372. It was used in the Roman Breviary after Compline from Easter Day until Trinity Sunday: "Queen of heaven, rejoice . . . and be glad . . . for the Lord has truly risen." See ALMA REDEMPTORIS MATER.

Reliquary (RELL-i-kwery; Latin *reliquiae*, remains). A receptacle for relics.

Reminiscere (rem-in-ISS-ker-ray; Latin, remember). The name of the second Sunday in Lent in medieval missals and in Lutheran use, from the first word of the Latin INTROIT for the day, "Remember, [O Lord, thy tender mercies]).

Repose, altar of. See ALTAR OF REPOSE.

Reproaches (Middle English from Latin *re*, back, *prope*, near: to bring back near). The singularly powerful PROSE of the Good Friday liturgy, drawn from Micah 6:3-4, in which God is heard rebuking the church for its faithlessness, "O my people, what have I done to you . . . ?"

Requiem (REK-we-em; Middle English from Latin *requiem*, after rest). A celebration of the Eucharist in connection with the Burial of the Dead. The name of this form of the mass derives from the first word of the INTROIT for the mass, "Rest (*requiem*) eternal grant them, O Lord."

Reredos (REER-doss; Middle English from Latin *retro*, backward, and *dorsum*, the back). The ornamented wall or screen of wood or stone behind an altar in the EASTWARD POSITION. The reredos is often embellished with carved figures or other decoration and POLYCHROME.

Reservation (Middle English from Latin *reservare*, to keep back). The practice of keeping ("reserving") some of the consecrated bread and wine from one celebration of the Holy Communion to the next for the purpose of communing those, such as the dying, who are in need of the Sacrament between celebrations of the Eucharist. See AUMBRY, SACRAMENT HOUSE, TABERNACLE.

Reserved sacrament. The consecrated eucharistic elements kept for the purpose of communing the sick. See AUMBRY, SACRAMENT HOUSE, TABERNACLE.

Responsive Prayer. The name in the *Lutheran Book of Worship* for the SUFFRAGES drawn by the nineteenth-century Lutheran liturgists from the medieval forms of Lauds and Vespers (the General Suffrages), from Prime (the Morning Suffrages), and from Compline (the Evening Suffrages). In the present Lutheran book there are two forms: **Responsive Prayer** 1, for use in the morning; **Responsive Prayer** 2, for use at other times (noon, afternoon, evening).

Responsorial psalmody. Psalms, such as the psalm between the first and second lesson in the Eucharist, sung by a single voice with a refrain by the choir or congregation.

Responsory (Middle English from Latin *respondere*, to respond). The proper (that is, variable according to the day or season) liturgical response to the readings in daily prayer, particularly Morning Prayer (Matins), in which Scripture verses are arranged so as to comment on the lesson just read. The responsory consists of the singing of a refrain after a brief series of verses. The traditional responsories at Matins are among the oldest and finest liturgical compositions and chants in the church's possession.

Responsum breve (re-SPON-sum BREV-ay; Latin, brief response). A short RESPONSORY used following the brief lesson (CHAPTER) in PRIME, the LITTLE HOURS, and COMPLINE, less complex than the responsory used in MATINS.

Retable (REE-table; Latin *retro-tabulum*, a back table). A GRADINE, a shelf or ledge behind and above the MENSA of the altar, designed to support the REREDOS.

Riddels (RID-ells; Old French *ridel*, a curtain). The tall curtains at the sides of an English-style altar, properly hung always at right angles to the DOSSAL.

Ring (Old English *hring*). With the PASTORAL STAFF and MITER, a principal part of the insignia of a bishop in the Roman Catholic and Episcopal churches.

Ripidion. See FAN.

Rite (Latin *ritus*, religious custom, usage). 1. An order of worship, such as the rite of burial. 2. The whole body of liturgical services according to the USE of a significant part of the church, such as the Lutheran rite.

Ritual (Latin *ritus*, religious custom, usage). The book containing the OCCASIONAL SERVICES that may be performed by parish clergy.

Robe (Middle English from Latin *rauba*, clothes taken as booty, robe). The preaching GOWN. The academic gown transplanted into church usage, worn in the eighteenth century in the Anglican church and brought to American Lutheran churches by Henry Melchior Muhlenberg, who had a clerical robe made in London after the English pattern. It became the standard vestment for Lutheran clergy in America until the middle of the twentieth century when it gave way to the CASSOCK, SURPLICE, and STOLE. It remains the most widely used vestment among the Reformed churches and elsewhere.

Rochet (ROW-shett; Middle English from Germanic *rok*, a coat). A white vestment like a SURPLICE, derived from the ALB, with narrow sleeves like the alb (or else sleeveless) and falling to near the floor like a surplice, now worn by bishops but originally worn by all clerics. A **winged rochet** is a sleeveless rochet with panels like wings falling from the shoulders to conceal the elbows from behind, but allowing freedom of movement.

Rogate (row-GAA-tay; Latin, ask). The name of the fifth Sunday after Easter in medieval missals and Lutheran use, deriving from the practice on the following three days of "asking" God's blessing on the fields, the ROGATION DAYS. The name is thus a departure from the practice of taking the name of a Sunday from the first word of the first proper, the INTROIT (see VOCEM JUCUNDITATIS).

Rogation Days (Middle English from Latin *rogare*, to ask, supplicate). Days of prayer and fasting for fruitful fields; the Major Rogation was on April 25, the Minor Rogation on the Monday, Tuesday, and Wednesday before Ascension Day. In the twentieth-century reform of the calendar, the Greater Litany on April 25 has been eliminated; the time and manner of observing the Lesser (i.e., established later) Litanies, like the EMBER DAYS, are in the Roman Catholic church left to the episcopal conferences. The *Book of Common Prayer* provides three sets of propers for the Rogation Days "for use on the traditional days or at other times": for fruitful seasons, for commerce and industry, for stewardship of creation. The *Lutheran Book of Worship* has made of the three Prayer Book sets one set of propers for the stewardship of creation.

Roman Breviary. The form of the daily office for the entire Roman church, published in 1570 and in use until the publication of the Liturgy of the Hours in 1970.

Roman missal. The MISSAL of the Roman church published in 1570 to supercede the various local medieval missals. It remained in use until the publication of the Roman sacramentary in 1969-1970.

Rood (RUDE; Old English *rod*, a rod, cross). 1. The cross. 2. The cross with the figure of Christ crucified, with the Blessed Virgin and St. John on either side, placed on or hung from a **rood beam** across the chancel arch of a Gothic church, or part of the **rood screen**. The **rood loft** was a GALLERY built over the entrance to the CHANCEL on which stood the rood cross with the figures of St. Mary and St. John, from which portions of the service were occasionally read. Later, the gallery was omitted and the rood loft or rood screen became a largely ornamental feature separating the NAVE and CHOIR.

Roodmass. May 3, the Feast of the Finding ("the Invention") of the HOLY CROSS.

Rorate (row-RAH-tay; Latin, drop down). The fourth Sunday in Advent, so called from the first word of the Latin INTROIT for the day, "Drop down, you heavens from above."

Rosary (ROSE-a-ree; Latin *rosarium*, a rose garden). A set of devotions to the fifteen mysteries of the Blessed Virgin; fifteen decades or groups of ten AVE MARIAS are recited, each preceded by an Our Father and followed by a GLORIA PATRI; the rosary is divided into three parts or chaplets, each containing five decades.

Rose (Old English from Latin *rosa*, red). 1. A symbol of Christ, drawn from the Song of Solomon 2:1 and set forth in the German carol *Es ist ein Ros entsprungen*, "Lo, how a rose is growing." 2. A symbol of the Virgin Mary.

Rose window. A circular window, the mullions of which form petal-like openings; usually found in the west front of Gothic cathedrals.

Rubric (ROO-brik; Middle English from Latin *ruber*, red). A direction for conducting the services of the church, often printed in red to distinguish the rubrics from the text of the service.

Rural dean. In the Church of England, the head of a group of parishes appointed by the bishop; an ancient office, revived in 1836.

Ss

Sabbath (Old English from Hebrew *shabbath*, rest). Saturday, the day of rest according to the commandment (Luke 23:56; Exodus 20:8-11). The name of the ancient holy day of the Hebrews was appropriated by certain Christian groups after the Reformation and transferred to Sunday, applying all the Old Testament legal proscriptions against work to the first day of the week, the day of resurrection.

Sacrament (Middle English from Latin *sacramentum*, a sacred obligation, military oath). An ordinary action which, given power by the word of God, distills the essence of the Gospel. In Christian history a great number of actions, as many as seventy, have been regarded as sacraments. In the late Middle Ages, seven sacraments were identified: Baptism, Confirmation, Penance, the Eucharist, Marriage, Ordination, and Anointing (Unction). The Lutheran tradition recognizes two, three, or four sacraments: Baptism and Holy Communion are universally so regarded; the Apology of the Augsburg Confession (XII) calls Absolution "a sacrament of penitence" and (XIII) allows Ordination, properly understood, to be called a sacrament. The Anglican Thirty-nine Articles call Baptism and the Supper of the Lord sacraments "ordained of Christ our Lord in the Gospel," and the other five actions "commonly called Sacraments . . . are not be counted for Sacraments of the Gospel."

Sacrament house. An elaborately carved receptacle of wood or stone, usually to the NORTH (Gospel) side of the altar, attached to the wall or freestanding, sometimes taking the shape of a great tower, popular in Germany as a place in which to reserve the Sacrament of the Altar so that it was available for taking to the sick.

Sacramental lights or **eucharistic lights**. The two candles on the altar of Anglican and Lutheran churches used at the celebration of the Holy Communion.

Sacramental linens. The CORPORAL, PURIFICATORS, PALL, and the veil when made of fine white linen rather than colored silk.

Sacramental vessels. Principally the CHALICE, CIBORIUM, and PATEN, but also CRUETS and FLAGONS.

Sacramentary (sak-ra-MEN-ter-ee; Middle English from Latin *sacramentum*, a sacred obligation, military oath). The liturgical book containing the text of the Eucharist and the PROPERS, but not the lessons nor those parts of the mass which are sung by the choir. The sacramentary was replaced in the tenth century by the MISSAL and the PONTIFICAL.

Sacrarium (sa-KRARE-ee-um; Latin, a place for keeping holy things). 1. A drain into the earth. See PISCINA. 2. The SANCTUARY or CHANCEL.

Sacring bell (SAY-kring bell; Middle English *sacringe*, consecrating, from Latin *sacrare*, to consecrate). A bell rung at the ELEVATION of the host during the GREAT THANKSGIVING.

Sacristan (Middle English from Latin *sacristanus*, one in charge of sacred vessels, *sacrista*). 1. One responsible for ecclesiastical property. 2. A sexton.

Sacristy (SAK-riss-tee; French *sacristie* from Latin *sacristia*, holy things). A room in a church used for keeping the sacred vessels and vestments and for the vesting of the ministers of the service. For convenience, especially when several ministers and servers are vesting at the same time, the sacristy should be spacious. Ideally, so that the ministers may be undisturbed in their devotional preparation for the service, there should be a separate **working sacristy** for those who prepare the paraments, sacramental vessels and elements, flowers.

Sacrosanctum concilium (sak-roe-SANK-tum con-SILL-ee-um; Latin, most holy council). The formal name of the Constitution on the Sacred Liturgy of the Second Vatican Council, promulgated December 4, 1963, by Pope Paul VI, outlining the agenda for liturgical reform and renewal that had wide influence beyond the Roman church.

Said service. A service that is entirely spoken, although sometimes enhanced by hymns, as opposed to a **sung service**, in which the text of the liturgy is sung or chanted. The two designations come from the past participial forms of the two verbs used to describe how a service or part of a service is to be voiced: "The minister sings or says. . . ." A recent Lutheran peculiarity is to refer to a "spoken service" rather than use the traditional phrase, "a said service."

Saint Peter's Chains. August 1. See LAMMAS.

Saint Peter's Chair. February 22. A feast on the Roman calendar honoring Peter as the head of the church, and his *cathedra* of episcopal authority and focus of church unity founded on the leader of the twelve apostles.

Sakkos (SAK-os; Greek, sack cloth). In the BYZANTINE RITE, a dalmatic worn instead of the PHELONION (chasuble) by bishops. The name derives from the sack cloth of garments worn by ascetics.

Saltire (Middle English from Latin *saltare*, to jump). Cross saltire, a heraldic designation for a St. Andrew's CROSS, the name deriving from an X-shaped animal barricade that people can jump over.

Salutation (Middle English from Latin *salutatio*, a greeting). The liturgical greeting, "The Lord be with you," with its response, "And also with you," is used to introduce prayers, benedictions, and other parts of the service. Originally it was used to renew the attention of the congregation before significant parts of the mass.

Salve regina [mater misericordiae] (SALL-way ray-GEE-na; Latin, Hail, queen, mother of mercy). One of four antiphons to the blessed Virgin Mary sung to conclude the daily office, attributed, among others, to Hermann Contractus (d. 1054): "Hail, holy queen, mother of mercy, our life, our sweetness, and our hope. . . ." In the Roman Breviary it was used from Trinity Sunday until Advent. It was a great favorite and is sung with intense devotion in many places still, including certain Swedish Lutheran monasteries. See *ALMA REDEMPTORIS MATER*.

Sanctuary (Middle English from Latin *sanctuarium*, a holy place). The area immediately surrounding an altar and, in older churches, enclosed within the communion or altar rail. Sanctuary is not properly a name for the interior of a church.

Sanctuary light or **sanctuary lamp**. A lamp hanging in or near the SANCTUARY to signify the presence of God in his temple. A red glass is used to signify the general divine presence; a clear glass is used to indicate the presence of the RESERVED SACRAMENT.

Sanctus (SAHNK-tus; Middle English from Latin, holy). The seraphim's song from Isaiah 6:3, "Holy, holy, holy Lord, God of power and might," used as part of the PREFACE in the GREAT THANKSGIVING. To the expanded text from Isaiah is added the BENEDICTUS QUI VENIT from Psalm 118:26 and Mark 11:9-10. Also called the **Seraphic Hymn**.

Sanctus Bell. See BELL, SANCTUS.

Sarum rite (SAIR-um; Old Sarum, Roman *Sorbiodunum*, city in Wiltshire, England, rebuilt nearby in the thirteenth century as New Sarum or Salisbury). The USE of Salisbury cathedral in England, a medieval modification of the Roman rite, formulated by Osmund (bishop, 1078-1099). By 1457, the rite had so spread that it was in use in nearly the whole of England, Wales, and Ireland.

Saturday of Our Lady. The association of Saturday with the Virgin Mary dates from medieval times as an extension of the association of Sunday with the Lord.

Savoy liturgy. The Reformed liturgy presented by Richard Baxter and other Puritans to the Savoy Conference in 1660 as a preferable alternative to the *Book of*

Common Prayer, characterized by prolixity and clericalization, the minister alone saying the long and clumsy service and the congregation simply listening to it.

Saxon alb. A white linen vestment, in appearance like a SURPLICE without sleeves, worn over the black robe or TALAR at celebrations of the Holy Communion. It is a German Lutheran version of the sleeveless ROCHET.

Scepter (Middle English from Greek *skeptron*, a stick, staff). An emblem of authority held by a sovereign on ceremonial occasions. A symbol of the universal authority of Christ the King.

Screen (Middle English from Middle Dutch *scherm*, a shield, protection). A division between the CHOIR and the NAVE. English screens were elaborately carved structures of wood or stone.

Scrutinies (Latin *scrutare*, to search, examine). The formalized testing and examination which candidates were required to undergo during Lent in the final stages of the preparation for Holy Baptism at Easter.

Second Vespers. Evening Prayer marking the conclusion of a festival that began with first Vespers on the eve of the day.

Secret. 1. The offertory prayer over the gifts in the Eucharist, so called because of its being said in a low voice by the priest in medieval rites. 2. Often **secreta**, the institution narrative, because it was said in a low voice; see MYSTERIUM.

Seder (SAY-der; Hebrew *sedher*, order, arrangement). The meal commemorating the deliverance of the Israelites from Egypt, celebrated on the eve of the first day of PASSOVER and again on the eve of the second day.

Sedia gestatoria (SAY-dee-a ghesta-TOR-ee-a; Latin). A portable throne on which the pope was carried by twelve footmen dressed in red, in order to make him more easily visible to the throngs of people through whom he was carried.

Sedilia (se-DEE-lee-a; Latin, a row of seats). Chairs or seats for the ministers of the service.

See (Middle English from Latin *sedes*, a seat, residence). The official seat of a bishop, the CATHEDRA, the chair, and hence the cathedral and city in which that seat is located; the center of jurisdiction and authority.

Septuagesima (sep-too-a-GHESS-i-ma; Latin, seventieth). The first Sunday of the now-suppressed season of PRE-LENT, being approximately seventy days before Easter. The lessons (1 Corinthians 9:24-10:5 and Matthew 20:1-16) dealt with the preparation of the vineyards at the spring equinox and were a kind of new year propers. In the monastic daily office the in-course reading of Genesis began on Septuagesima, reinforcing the new year theme.

Sequence (Latin *sequens*, following). A hymn sung on certain festivals between the second lesson and the Gospel as an elaboration of the final alleluia of the VERSE, to cover the moving of the book of the Gospels to the midst of the congregation where it is proclaimed. In the medieval period, the number and use of these hymns proliferated until nearly every Sunday and holy day had a proper sequence (see HYMN OF THE DAY); in the 1570 Roman missal, there were only four: *DIES IRAE* (in masses for the dead), *LAUDA SION SALVATOREM* (for CORPUS CHRISTI), *VENI, SANCTE SPIRITUS* (for Pentecost), and *VICTIMAE PASCHALI* (for Easter Day). Two sequences remain in present Roman Catholic and Lutheran use: on Easter, *Victimae Paschali* ("Christians to the Paschal victim"); on Pentecost in the Roman rite, *Veni, Sancte Spiritus*, but in the Lutheran rite, *VENI, CREATOR SPIRITUS*, "Come, Holy Ghost, our souls inspire."

Sermon (Middle English from Latin *sermo*, conversation, discourse). The exposition of a scriptural text addressed by a preacher to a congregation, connecting the proclamation of the Bible with contemporary experience and situations. Evasive substitutes such as "meditation" or "message," betraying an insecurity and a discomfort with traditional use and practice, are to be scrupulously avoided.

Serve. A verb avoided by careful users of the English language in such expressions as "The Holy Communion will be served Sunday at 10:00." The Sacrament is more than a meal set before diners. It is a remembrance by which the past is made present and the presence of Christ is effected and acclaimed. The verb properly used to acknowledge and express the richness of this meal is *celebrate*. One does not serve the Eucharist, but one may serve at the celebration of the Eucharist.

Server (Middle English from Latin *servus*, a slave). One who assists the ministers of a service. See ACOLYTE.

Service of the Word. 1. The liturgy of the word as the first half of the Eucharist. 2. A service of readings and preaching, like the ancient SYNAXIS, without the celebration of the Holy Communion, included in the *Lutheran Book of Worship*.

Seven. See NUMBER SYMBOLISM.

Sexagesima (sex-a-GHESS-i-ma; Latin sixtieth). The second Sunday of PRE-LENT, being approximately sixty days before Easter. The lessons (2 Corinthians 11:19-12:9 and Luke 8:4-15) dealt with the sowing of the seed at the spring equinox and are new year propers like those of SEPTUAGESIMA.

Sext (Latin *sexta*, sixth). The noonday office in the Liturgy of the Hours, prayed at the sixth hour of the Roman day.

Sexton (SEX-ten; Middle English from Latin *sacristanus*, one in charge of sacred vessels). A layperson who has the care of a church building and property. See SACRISTAN, from which the noun sexton is derived.

Shape notes. A device originated by William Little and William Smith in *The Easy Instructor* (1801) in which the shape of the note heads on the staff corresponded with the four solmization syllables: a triangle note for *fa*, oval for *sol*, square for *la*, diamond for *mi*.

Shema (shem-AH; Hebrew, hear). An affirmation of monotheism and the central liturgical confession of Judaism, from Deuteronomy 6:4, "Hear, O Israel, the Lord is our God, the Lord alone."

Ship. In Scandinavian churches, a model sailing ship is often suspended from the ceiling, reflecting the Viking seafaring tradition and suggesting the image of the church as the ark of salvation.

Shrove Tuesday (Old English *scrifan*, to write, prescribe [penance]). The day before Ash Wednesday, on which it was the custom to be shriven or absolved from one's sins in preparation for the Great Fast.

Sidesman. In the Anglican church, assistants to the church wardens, whose responsibility it is to ensure attendance of parishioners at services of the church, promote the cause of religion in the parish, and assist the church wardens. The office derives from assistants appointed by the bishop in every parish anciently to guard against heresy and irregularity.

Signation (sig-NAY-shun; Old French from Latin *signare*, to mark with a sign). The signing with the cross, especially in Holy Baptism when the new child of God is "sealed by the Holy Spirit and marked with the cross of Christ forever."

Silence (Latin *silens*, silent). A time of deep corporate stillness and contemplation in the absence of all words, actions, music, sound, and movement was recovered in the liturgical churches in the twentieth century as a welcome period of deep and tranquil communion in a restless and busy world. The principal times for such silence are before the collect or Prayer of the Day, after the sermon, and after communion before the benediction. They are an integral part of the liturgy and should be of increasing length and depth as the fullness of God's generous goodness and grace is progressively revealed in the Eucharist. Silence is also appropriate after each psalm in daily prayer.

Simnel (Middle English from Latin *simila*, fine flour). A cake, according to English custom, made of flour, yeast, saffron, currants, and spice, to be taken to mothers on the fourth Sunday of Lent, called MOTHERING SUNDAY.

Simon. See APOSTLES' SYMBOLS.

Sintflutgebet (SINT-floot-ge-bate; German, flood prayer). Luther's version of the prayer of thanksgiving for baptism said over the water in the celebration of Holy Baptism, recalling the great biblical uses of water as an agent of cleansing, renewal, and life.

Skufya. A Russian name for the black pointed cap worn by priests in the Eastern church. It corresponds to the BIRETTA of Western churches.

Solemnity (Middle English from Latin *sollemnis*, stated, established, appointed). In the Roman Catholic calendar one of the days of greatest importance, beginning with first Vespers of the preceding day and on which both the GLORIA IN EXCELSIS and the creed are said. Solemnities are celebrated on their assigned days, and no other masses can take their place.

Sounding board (Middle English from Latin *sonus*, sound). A roof suspended over a pulpit to assist in the projection of the preacher's voice. Such a canopy gives a finished appearance to the pulpit, adds to its dignity, and is most desirable.

South (Old English *suth*). The EPISTLE SIDE of an altar or chancel, the right side as one faces the altar from the nave.

Spear (Old English *spere*). 1. In the Eastern churches, a small dagger-like instrument used to cut particles from the altar bread.

2. In the West, a symbol of the passion of Christ.

Species (Latin, an appearance, likeness). Either of the consecrated elements of the Holy Communion. See KIND.

Spoken service. See SAID SERVICE.

Sponge. Used in the Eastern churches to brush particles from the PATEN into the CHALICE and to wipe the chalice after communion.

Spoon (Old English *spon*, a chip of wood). 1. The utensil made of precious metal with a perforated gold-lined bowl, used to remove foreign particles which may fall into the wine in the CHALICE. 2. In the Eastern churches, the Holy Communion is administered to the laity by means of a spoon, the consecrated bread having been mingled with the consecrated wine in the chalice, so that both KINDS or SPECIES are received together. In the Western church, a spoon is sometimes used to administer the Sacrament under the form of wine to the infirm who cannot receive the bread or drink from a cup.

Squint. See HAGIOSCOPE.

Stabat mater dolorosa (STAH-bat MA-tare DOE-la-ro-sa; Latin, the sorrowful mother stood [at the cross]). A hymn for Holy Week, of unknown authorship, dating from the late twelfth century, describing most movingly the sorrowful mother at the cross of her son. It only gradually came into the services of the church, and entered the Roman missal as a SEQUENCE and the Roman Breviary as an OFFICE HYMN in 1727.

Stall (Old English *steal*, a standing place, compartment). A fixed seat for the clergy or choir.

Standing (Old English *standan*). The ancient posture for prayer. See ORANS.

Star (Old English *steorre*). A symbol of Christ, the morning star and the daystar (2 Peter 1:19; Revelation 22:16). A **five-pointed** star is usually used to recall the sign given to the MAGI. A **six-pointed** star, the star of David, is called the Creator's star, from the six days of creation. A **seven-pointed** star, usually with a letter in each point, enumerates the seven gifts of the Holy Spirit (Isaiah 11:2 in the Vulgate): *sapientia* (wisdom), *intellectus* (understanding), *consilium* (counsel), *fortitudo* (might), *scientia* (knowledge), *pietas* (piety), *timor Dei* (fear of God). An **eight-pointed** star is a symbol of regeneration.

Star cover or **asterisk** (Greek, little star). In the Byzantine rite, a domed cover in the shape of a cross with a small star or cross hanging from the intersection, placed over the paten to support the veil so that it will not touch the holy bread.

Station (Middle English from Latin *statio*, a standing still). A stop or a pause in a procession while

prayer is said as, for example, at the CRÈCHE in a procession on Christmas or before the altar at the conclusion of the Palm Sunday procession.

Station collect. A prayer said at a STATION in a procession.

Station days. 1. A fixed feast on which the bishop of Rome celebrated mass in a particular church in his city. The station days have left an impress on the propers for certain saints' days. 2. The fast days of Wednesday and Friday.

Stational churches. Churches in Rome and its suburbs where the pope celebrated mass on the various days of the year. In the fifth century there were eighty-nine days in the cycle, with stations at forty-three churches. Among the most famous were Santa Maria Maggiore on the First Sunday in Advent, the first and third masses of Christmas Day, and Easter Day; St. John Lateran on Holy Saturday; and Santa Sabina on Ash Wednesday.

Stations of the cross. A series of crosses, usually with a pictorial representation, arranged around the interior of a church so that people may perform a pilgrimage within the confines of the building, pausing at each STATION for a brief devotion on the successive stages of Christ's passion, death, and burial. The number of stations has varied from seven to thirty or more; in the eighteenth and nineteenth centuries, the number was fixed at fourteen: 1. Jesus is condemned to death; 2. Jesus receives his cross; 3. Jesus falls the first time; 4. Jesus meets his mother; 5. Simon of Cyrene is compelled to carry the cross; 6. a woman (Veronica) wipes the face of Jesus; 7. Jesus falls the second time; 8. Jesus meets the women of Jerusalem; 9. Jesus falls the third time; 10. Jesus is stripped of his garments; 11. Jesus is nailed to the cross; 12. Jesus dies on the cross; 13. Jesus' body is taken down from the cross; 14. Jesus is laid in the tomb. Also called the **Way of the Cross**.

Stephen. A common symbol for the first martyr is a coat surrounded by three stones, indicating the manner of his death (Acts 6:8-7:60).

Stikarion (Greek *stichos*, rank, row). The deacon's vestment in the BYZANTINE RITE; a long, straight vestment with wide sleeves, similar to the Western DALMATIC.

Stock (Old English *stocc*, tree trunk). A container, usually a metal cylinder with a tight-fitting top, in which oil is carried for anointing.

Stole (Old English from Greek *stole*, a long robe). A scarf of fabric in the liturgical color worn over the shoulders by ordained ministers. The origin of the stole is uncertain, but the stole, as a large towel, preeminently the badge of a servant, has been the distinctive vestment of the deacon, who wears it like a sash over the left shoulder and fastened under the right arm. The knee-length preaching stole is worn with the SURPLICE; the longer, ankle-length stole is worn with the ALB. The traditional prayer while vesting makes the stole a symbol of immortality, lost by Adam but restored by Christ: "Restore to me, Lord, the robe of immortality which I lost by the sin (*praevaricatione*) of the first parent, and, although unworthy, I draw near to your sacred mystery, may I nonetheless be found worthy of everlasting joy." In Eastern use, the wide stole of the priest is joined in the front for its entire length (see EPITRAKELION); the long deacon's stole is called an ORARION, the bishop's stole an OMOPHORION.

Stoup (STOOP; Middle English *stowp*, a vessel, pail). A basin for holy water at the entrance of a church to serve as a reminder of Holy Baptism.

Stowe missal. An early mass book of the Irish church, dated some time after 792, once preserved at Stowe House in Bucks. It contains extracts from John's Gospel, and ordinary and canon of the mass, propers for three separate masses, Holy Baptism, the visitation of the sick, a treatise in Irish on the ceremonies of the mass, and three Irish spells.

Stripping of the altar. The ceremonial removal of all ornaments, candles, and cloths from the altar at the conclusion of the Eucharist on Maundy Thursday. Originally a simply practical matter so that the altar could be washed in preparation for the Easter celebration, the practice took on symbolic importance and suggested the stripping of the body of Jesus of his clothing, power, and glory by his captors.

Subcinctorium (sub-sink-TOR-ee-um; Latin, beneath the cincture). A papal vestment, consisting of a cloth ornamented with the AGNUS DEI at the lower end, attached to a separate CINCTURE or girdle and hanging at the pope's right side. It is related to the Byzantine EPIGONATION, and both derive from the MANIPLE, originally a hygenic cloth attached to the waist.

Subdeacon (Middle English from Latin *subdiaconus*, subdeacon). 1. The highest of the minor orders of the medieval church. 2. A second assisting minister, after the deacon, at a solemn mass; the person whose task it is to read the EPISTLE.

Submersion (Latin *submergere*, to plunge under, immerse). A mode of baptism in which the candidate's body is plunged entirely beneath the water. It is the mode of baptism in the Eastern churches and in the AMBROSIAN RITE, and in a different form, the mode employed in those Protestant churches like the Baptist church that practice adult baptism instead of infant baptism.

Sudary (SUE-da-ree; Latin *sudarium*, a handkerchief, from *sudor*, sweat). The OFFERING VEIL.

Suffrages (SUFF-ra-ghez; Middle English from Latin *suffragia*, petitions). Short petitions in a prayer; specifically, in the *Lutheran Book of Worship*, the two forms of RESPONSIVE PRAYER, which bear the subtitle Suffrages, their name in previous Lutheran books.

Sunday of the Passion. The Sunday before Easter Day, popularly called PALM SUNDAY, that begins the solemn contemplation of the passion and death of Christ during HOLY WEEK. The primary characteristic of the Sunday is the reading or chanting of the passion account in the Gospel of the current year of the lectionary cycle.

Sung service. See SAID SERVICE.

Superfrontal (Latin, over the frontal). A band of fabric that extends across the front of an altar from the MENSA to the depth of a handspan, the primary purpose of which is to conceal the means of the suspension of the frontal. Now it is often used without a frontal beneath it. See FRONTLET.

Super populum (Latin, over the people). A prayer of blessing said over the people at the conclusion of mass. The LEONINE SACRAMENTARY provided a *super populum* for every mass; the GREGORIAN SACRAMENTARY restricted the practice to the weekdays of Lent. The present Roman rite and the Episcopal *Book of Occasional Services* provide such prayers over the people for the Sundays and weekdays of Lent.

Supplices te (SOUP-li-kess tay; Latin, we beseech you). The ninth section of the Roman CANON, a later addition to the original stratum, beginning "We humbly beseech you, almighty God." The prayer is that the offering be carried to heaven so that those who communicate at the earthly altar may be filled with all heavenly benediction and grace.

Supra quae (SOUP-ra kwhy; Latin, upon which). The eighth section of the Roman CANON, part of the earlier stratum, beginning "Upon which look with favor and accept," remembering God's acceptance of the offerings of Abel, Abraham, and Melchizedek.

Surge, illuminare (SUR-gay il-LOOM-in-a-ray; Latin, rise, shine). The third song of Isaiah (Isaiah 60:1-3, 11a, 14c, 18-19); Canticle 11 in Morning Prayer, Rite II in the *Book of Common Prayer.*

Surplice (SIR-pliss; Middle English from Latin *super*, over, and *pellicum*, a fur coat). A graceful knee- or ankle-length white vestment worn over the cassock by ministers of the service, whether ordained or not. Its ample proportions derive from its use over a fur undergarment in unheated northern European churches. The surplice is appropriate for the daily prayer offices and for use as a choir vestment.

Sursam corda (SUR-sahm COR-dah; Latin, upwards the hearts). The verses which introduce the PREFACE dialogue and which are of the greatest antiquity, reaching back at least into the second century. Later the salutation, "The Lord be with you," and its response, "And also with you," were added to the *sursam corda* to call the congregation's attention to the beginning of the GREAT THANKSGIVING; in the LITURGY OF ST. JOHN CHRYSOSTOM, the Apostolic Greeting, "The grace of our Lord Jesus Christ . . . ," introduces the *sursam corda* verses.

Symbol (Greek *sunbolon*, a seal, signet ring, legal bond or warrant, from *sunballein*, to throw together, compare). A name used beginning in the fourth or fifth century, in the East and West, for the declaratory creeds, especially the Apostles' Creed, perhaps suggesting the pact made between the baptismal candidate and God, but more probably deriving from the baptismal confession of faith as a sign and symbol of belief in the triune God.

Synaxis (SIN-ak-sis; Greek, assembly). Any assembly for worship. In the West, synaxis was used as a name for a non-eucharistic service of psalms, lessons, and prayers which gave rise to the DIVINE OFFICE and to the Liturgy of the Word (ante-communion).

Syriac breviary or Calendar of Antioch. The oldest extant martyrology, composed between 362 and 381.

Tabernacle (Middle English from Latin *tabernaculum*, a tent). A freestanding safe for the Sacrament, which was placed on the altar of Roman Catholic and certain Anglican and Lutheran churches as a focus of devotion. With the reforms of the liturgy begun by the Second Vatican Council that encouraged the celebration of the Eucharist facing the people across the altar, the tabernacle could no longer occupy its place on the altar between the presiding minister and the congregation, nor was it appropriate behind the presiding minister whose back would be turned to it. The tabernacle therefore is now kept in a chapel or space of its own.

Talar (ta-LAR; Latin *talaria*, skirts). The black GOWN of European clergy, deriving from the cassock.

Tantum ergo sacramentum. The beginning of the two-stanza doxology of Thomas Aquinas' Latin hymn on the sacrament of Holy Communion, PANGE, LINGUA, GLORIOSI CORPORIS MYSTERIUM, sung as a separate hymn at benediction of the Blessed Sacrament. See BENEDICTION 2.

Tau cross. See CROSS.

Te Deum [laudamus] (tay DAY-um; Latin, [we praise] you, God). The ancient creedlike canticle of praise, the church's great song of thanksgiving, "You are God, we praise you." A Latin hymn in rhythmic prose, it is a Western relative of the GLORIA IN EXCELSIS, the structure of which it parallels. A pleasant tradition imagines that it was composed jointly and spontaneously by St. Ambrose and St. Augustine at the latter's baptism. It is Canticles 7 and 21 in Morning Prayer in the *Book of Common Prayer* and is part of the PASCHAL BLESSING in Morning Prayer in the *Lutheran Book of Worship*. It is also used as an independent song of thanksgiving.

Te igitur (tay IG-a-toor; Latin, [we pray] you, therefore). The opening words of the Roman CANON following the proper preface and the name of its first section, beginning "Wherefore, most merciful Father, we humbly pray and ask that you accept and bless these gifts. . . ."

Tenebrae (TEN-a-bray; Latin, shadows). A Holy Week service of Morning Prayer (Matins) sung by anticipation the evening before, during which fourteen psalms are sung. As each psalm is sung, another of fifteen candles on a HEARSE is extinguished until one remains. The remaining light is carried out of the church or hidden from view behind the altar during the singing of the morning GOSPEL CANTICLE (BENEDICTUS [DOMINUS DEUS]) and Psalm 51. Then a loud noise is made, and the single candle is brought back into view to signify the resurrection. All leave in silence. The service reflects an undesirable misuse of the Liturgy of the Hours, praying Morning Prayer at night ahead of its proper time to get it taken care of, a custom no longer tolerated.

Terce (TERSE; Latin *tertia*, third). The first of the LITTLE HOURS of daily prayer, said about nine o'clock in the morning, the third hour of the Roman day.

Tester (Latin *testerium*, a headpiece, from *testa*, head). A cloth, wood, or stone canopy. It is a sign of honor placed over an ALTAR, a CATHEDRA, a FONT. See BALDACHINO.

Theotokos (th-ee-oh-TOK-oss; Greek, God bearer). An ancient title of the Virgin Mary as the bearer of God, widely used in the Eastern churches and corresponding to the more usual Western title *Mater Dei*, mother of God.

This is the feast. See WORTHY IS CHRIST.

Thomas. See APOSTLES' SYMBOLS.

Three. See NUMBER SYMBOLISM.

Throne. In certain churches, when the altar is in the EASTWARD POSITION (against or near the wall), an elevated step in the center of the RETABLE or GRADINE on which the cross stands. It is an often unwitting recollection of a TABERNACLE (although the tabernacle was required to be a freestanding structure and not do double duty as a stand for the crucifix).

Thurible (THUR-i-bl; Middle English from Latin *thus*, incense). A container in which incense is burned. See CENSER.

Thurifer (THUR-i-fer; Latin, incense carrier). One who carries the THURIBLE in procession.

Tippet (TIP-it; Middle English *tipet*). A broad black scarf worn over the SURPLICE in Anglican churches, perhaps once part of the hood. In the eighteenth century the tippet was worn with a black robe, and while in London, Henry Melchior Muhlenberg adopted such a gown and tippet for his use and introduced it to Lutheran churches in America.

Todah (toe-DAH). A genre of Jewish thanksgiving, consisting of an account of the works of God and a petition that the prayers of Israel may be heard. The *todah* has been proposed as the source of the Jewish BERAKAH and of the Christian GREAT THANKSGIVING.

Todtenfest (German, festival of the departed). A service of commemoration of all the faithful departed observed in German lands after the Reformation on

December 31, the last day of the civil year, or on the last Sunday after Trinity (Pentecost), the last day of the church year.

Tone (Middle English from Latin *tonus*, a sound, tone). A melodic formula designed to accommodate texts of varying length and pattern of accent, useful for singing assigned readings, prayers, psalms, and canticles.

Tonus peregrinus (TONE-us pe-ri-GREEN-us; Latin, wandering, foreign, or pilgrim tone). A psalm tone with two dominant or reciting notes for the first and second halves of the chant, thus giving the effect of a wandering of the voice from the ordinary pitch of recitation. The *tonus peregrinus* was used with Psalm 114 (*In exitu Israel*) in Sunday Vespers; it was also traditionally the preferred tone to which the MAGNIFICAT was sung.

Torches. Candles fitted to a staff so that they may be carried in procession. For outdoor processions, the candles should be shielded by a glass chimney.

Tract (Latin *tractim*, without ceasing). Verses of Scripture which form part of the traditional GRADUAL, taking the place of the ALLELUIA during Lent when alleluia is put away. The name derives from the way it was sung—long and drawn out.

Transept (TRAN-sept; new Latin, cross partition). A crosswise extension of a church building, originally added to provide more space on either side of the altar.

Transfiguration (Middle English from Latin *transfigurare*, to change form). The commemoration of the transfiguration of Christ, described in Matthew 17:1-8; Mark 9:2-8; Luke 9:28-36, is traditionally observed on August 6. In Lutheran practice, recognizing the role of the event as a preview of the glory of Christ given before the onset of the passion, the transfiguration is observed annually on the last Sunday after the Epiphany. In Roman practice, the event is the focus of the second Sunday in Lent.

Transubstantiation (tran-sub-stan-she-A-shun). The transformation and conversion of the substance of the bread and wine of the Eucharist into the body and blood of Christ, only the accidents (appearance, taste, smell) of bread and wine remaining. The doctrine was developed in the late Middle Ages based on the metaphysics of Aristotle.

Trefoil (TREE-foil). A stylized form of a clover leaf with its three lobes, a symbol of the Holy Trinity; sometimes seen in conjunction with an equilateral **triangle**.

Triduum (TRIDD-oo-um; Latin *triduum sacrum*, sacred three days). The three-day celebration of the central events of Christianity, the passion, death, and resurrection of Christ, celebrated from Maundy Thursday evening through Holy Saturday, culminating in the EASTER VIGIL.

Trikirion (try-KEER-ee-on; Greek, three candles). A three-branched candlestick, held in the right hand by bishops of the BYZANTINE RITE when blessing the people. See DIKIRION.

Triptych (TRIP-tick; Greek *triptukhos*, threefold). A picture or icon with half-doors attached to its outer edges, so that, when shut, the picture is completely covered for protection or for austerity, as during Lent.

Trisagion (triss-AHG-ee-on; Greek, thrice-holy). "Holy God, holy mighty, holy immortal, have mercy on us," a regular feature of the liturgies of the Eastern churches. The Trisagion is used after the Old Testament lesson in the liturgy of the Lutheran church in India and appears in a slightly amended form in the *Lutheran Book of Worship* at the beginning of RESPONSIVE PRAYERS 1 and 2. In the *Book of Common Prayer*, it is an alternative to the Kyrie in the Eucharist.

Troparion (trow-PAR-e-on). In the Eastern church, a stanza of religious poetry often applied to the *apolytikion*, the troparion of the day.

Trope (TROWP; Greek *tropos*, a way, manner, turn). A word or phrase interpolated as an embellishment of the text of the mass or the BREVIARY office sung by the choir. The oldest known collection of such pieces dates from the tenth century. Tropes lost popularity during the thirteenth century and fell into disuse.

Troper (TROW-per). Originally a collection of TROPES; later used of a book of SEQUENCES.

Tunicle (TUNE-i-kel; Middle English from Latin *tunicula*, a little tunic). The vestment worn by the subdeacon (and crucifer) at the Eucharist, distinguished from the DALMATIC of the deacon by having only one crossbar on its decoration. The tunicle is a shorter form of the *tunica talaris* or *tunica alba*, which about the sixth century came to be worn by those in minor orders.

Turret (Middle English from Old French *tourete*, a little tower). A small hollow tower generally designed to enclose a circular staircase.

Uu

Unction (UNK-shun; Middle English from Latin *unguere*, to anoint). Anointing with oil, especially in the ministry of healing. **Extreme unction** is the old name for the anointing on the extremities of the body, now called the anointing of the sick, its focus now on healing rather than on the last rites in preparation for death.

Unde et memores (UN-day et mem-OR-rays; Latin, wherefore remembering [Lord]). The seventh section and part of the earlier stratum of the Roman CANON, beginning "Wherefore, Lord, we your servants as also your holy people remembering the blessed passion of Christ. . . ."

Undercroft (Middle English from Latin *crupta*, vault). A finished space beneath a church, technically below ground level.

Universal priesthood. The priesthood into which all the baptized have been admitted by virtue of their baptism (1 Peter 2:9; Exodus 19:6), the obligation and privilege of which is to offer the sacrifice of thanksgiving by presenting oneself for God's service, assisting those in need, and praying for all the world. The Christian ministry of the Gospel, the ministry of the word and sacraments, does not derive from this universal priesthood but from the requirement of the word of God for ministers to proclaim it in speech and in visible words, the sacraments.

Use (Middle English from Latin *uti*, to use). 1. The body of ceremonies, customs, and usages employed by a church in a particular place. 2. A particular custom that prevails in a certain place.

Vacant day. A day with no special propers appointed for it.

Veil (Middle English from Latin *velum*, a covering, veil). A cloth covering for the chalice and paten, made of white linen or of silk in the color of the day or season, removed at the OFFERTORY and replaced after communion. The linen veil used in Lutheran churches is often large enough to cover the FLAGONS as well as the chalice and paten, all of which is sometimes placed on the altar before the Holy Communion takes place. The **prayer of the veil** is a prayer said as the elements of the Eucharist are unveiled at the offertory; also called the SECRET, offertory prayer, or prayer over the gifts.

Veni, creator spiritus (VAY-nee kray-AH-tor SPEAR-i-toose; Latin, Come, creator spirit). The classic Christian hymn, of unknown authorship, traditionally prominent in all the great services of the church. The hymn to the Holy Spirit probably was written in the ninth century and is found from the tenth century on in the daily office for Pentecost and from the eleventh century at ordinations, dedications of churches, at the opening of synods, and other services. It was translated by Luther as *Komm, Gott Schoepfer, heiliger Geist*, by John Cosin as "Come, Holy Ghost, our souls inspire," and by John Dryden as "Creator Spirit, by whose aid."

Veni, Sancte Spiritus [et emitte coelitus] (VAY-nee SANK-tay SPEAR-i-toose; Latin, Come, Holy Spirit). The "golden SEQUENCE," a masterpiece of Latin hymnody in five stanzas of unknown authorship, found in manuscripts from 1200. It was originally appointed for use on weekdays of WHITSUNWEEK and was one of the four sequences retained in the Roman missal of 1570, appointed for Pentecost and the week following. It is found in many English translations.

Veni Sancte Spiritus, reple (VAY-nee SANK-tay SPEAR-i-toose, REH-play; Latin, Come Holy Spirit, fill [the hearts of the faithful]). A Pentecost antiphon found in an eleventh-century manuscript: "Come, Holy Spirit; fill the hearts of the faithful and kindle in them the fire of your love."

Venite [exultemus] (ven-EE-tay eks-ul-TAY-moose, or in British use, ve-NIGHT-ee; Latin, Come,

126

let us exult). Verses from Psalm 95 used as the invitational song of praise at the beginning of Morning Prayer, "Come, let us sing to the Lord."

Verba institutionis or **verba testamenti.** The words of blessing (as Luther called them in his *Formula missae, verba benedictionis*) spoken by Jesus at the institution of the Lord's Supper, together with their surrounding narration as used in the GREAT THANKSGIVING, "In the night in which he was betrayed. . . ." Usually abbreviated to **verba.**

Vere dignum (very DIG-num). The beginning of the PREFACE in the Roman CANON, beginning "It is truly fitting and right. . . ."

Verger (VERGE-er; Middle English from Latin *virga*, a rod). The officer who carries a mace or verge before a dignitary, originally to make way through a crowd. In the SARUM RITE the verger headed the procession. The term is now used for one who cares for the interior of a church building.

Verona sacramentary. See LEONINE SACRAMENTARY.

Verse (Old English from Latin *versus*, a furrow, line, verse). A brief biblical passage, usually assigned to the choir or cantor, sung after the second lesson as a preparation for the Gospel. Except in Lent, the verse begins with the Easter song, alleluia, and therefore is often called the **alleluia verse.**

Versicle (Latin *versiculus*, a little verse). A brief responsive verse or verses, usually from the psalms, employed in the services of the church.

Vesper lights. Branched candlesticks used for the office of Vespers in the Western church, as distinct from eucharistic lights, single candlesticks used in pairs at mass. See CANDLES.

Vespers (Latin *vesper*, the evening). Evening Prayer, the hour of daily prayer prayed at sunset; with Morning Prayer, one of the two principal hours of daily prayer. Vespers is used without an article: not "a Vespers."

Vestments (Middle English from Latin *vestimentum*, a garment). 1. The clothing worn by those who minister in the services of the church. 2. The coverings for the altar, which is often treated as a person—Christ, whom the altar represents.

Vestry (VESS-tree; Middle English from Latin *vestarium*, a wardrobe). The place for vesting. Later, a place for meeting, and then the body which met in the vestry, a church council.

Vexilla regis prodeunt (vex-ILL-ah RAY-ghiss PROD-ay-unt). A processional Latin hymn by Venantius Fortunatus (530-609), written for use at the solemn reception of a relic of the Holy Cross at a monastery in Poitiers, impressively drawing on a rich supply of imagery associated with the tree of the cross. The hymn is known in English in John Mason Neale's translation, "The royal banners forward go."

Viaticum (vee-AT-i-cum; Latin, provision for a journey). The Holy Communion given as food to strengthen one near death for the journey from this world to the next.

Vicar (VIK-er; Middle English from Latin *vicarius*, a substitute). One who serves in place of another, a deputy. In Anglican use, one who serves in place of the rector of a parish; in Lutheran use, often an intern, a seminarian who serves a parish, assisting the pastor in order to gain practical experience; in European Lutheran use, an assistant pastor.

Victimae paschali (VIK-tim-eye pas-KAL-ee; Latin, of the Paschal victim). A SEQUENCE ascribed to Wipo (ca. 1000-1050), appointed for Easter. It is an example of the transition from rhythmical but unrhymed sequences to the regular rhyming sequences, and it by its dramatization of the Easter event encouraged the development of the drama.

Vidi Aquam. See ASPERGES.

Vigil (Middle English from Latin *vigilia*, a night spent in watching). The eve of a feast when anciently the church would watch through the night in preparation for the dawning day. The *Lutheran Book of Worship* appoints three vigils, one for each of the three great festivals of the church year: the Vigil of Christmas, the Great Vigil of Easter, and the Vigil of Pentecost. The *Book of Common Prayer* appoints the Great Vigil of Easter and the Vigil of Pentecost.

Vigil light. A small candle left burning in a church as a visible testimony to a prayer that has been offered there and as a reminder and encouragement to those who come after.

Vinea facta est (VIN-ee-a FAC-ta est; Latin, [my beloved] had a vineyard). The Song of the Vineyard from Isaiah 5:1-2b, 7a, sung following the eighth lesson (Isaiah 4:2-4) in the Easter Vigil in the Lutheran rite and the Roman rite before 1955, beginning "I will sing for my beloved my love song about his vineyard."

Violet. The liturgical color used in seasons of repentance such as Lent.

Virgins. Those holy women (men were not commemorated in this category) remembered on the Christian calendar because of their renunciation of the world and their adherence to the celibate model of Christ.

Visigothic rite. See MOZARABIC RITE.

Visitation. The feast, now celebrated on May 31, commemorating the visit paid by the Virgin Mary to her relative Elizabeth during their mutual pregnancies, reported in Luke 1:39-47. The occasion was the setting for the song of Mary, the MAGNIFICAT. Before the calendar reforms beginning in 1969, the Visitation of the Blessed Virgin Mary was observed on July 2 on the Roman and Lutheran calendars.

Vocem jucunditatis (VO-chem you-cun-di-TAH-tis). The name given in medieval missals and certain Lutheran use to the fifth Sunday after Easter, also called ROGATE, from the first words of the INTROIT for the day, "With a voice of singing [declare ye, and tell this]."

Votum (VOH-tum; Latin, a prayer). 1. In the Lutheran Common Service (1888), the *Common Service Book*, the *Service Book and Hymnal*, and in German Lutheran use, an apostolic blessing from Philippians 4:7, said by the minister at the conclusion of the sermon. 2. In Roman Catholic theology the intention, not necessarily explicit, to use the sacraments of the church, although deprived of the opportunity to do so.

Washing the hands. The essential utilitarian act done before vesting and given symbolic significance exemplified in the traditional prayer, "Lord, give virtue to my hands, washing away every stain, so that I may be enabled to serve you without defilement of mind or body." The prayer is the first of the seven prayers while vesting, the six others relating to each of the EUCHARISTIC VESTMENTS.

Watch night. A designation for New Year's Eve introduced by the Methodist church as an occasion for religious services to temper the excesses of the secular celebration.

Waters, blessing of. See BLESSING OF THE WATERS.

Way of the Cross. See STATIONS OF THE CROSS.

Week of Prayer for Christian Unity. A weeklong emphasis on the unity of the church, observed yearly from January 18 (in the *Book of Common Prayer* and in the *Lutheran Book of Worship*, the Confession of St. Peter) through January 25 (the Conversion of St. Paul). The week was first observed in 1908; in 1935, Abbe Paul Courtier invited all Christians to join in a common observance of a week of prayer for Christian unity, and the Commission on Faith and Order of the World Council of Churches endorsed the project. The *Lutheran Book of Worship* is the only service book to include the week on its calendar, although it is widely observed throughout Christianity.

West. 1. That part of a longitudinal church building opposite the chancel and altar, regardless of the compass direction. The **west front** is the facade and usually the principal entrance to a church. 2. The churches deriving from the western part of the Roman Empire, dominated by Rome, as opposed to the churches of the East, having their focus in Constantinople.

West Syrian. The most widely found pattern of the ANAPHORA (also called Antiochene or Syro-Antiochene) in the Liturgies of St. John Chrysostom, St. Basil, St. James, the *Apostolic Constitutions*, and standardized by the fourth century: (1) SURSAM CORDA, (2) PREFACE, (3) pre-Sanctus, (4) SANCTUS, (5) post-Sanctus, (6) institution narrative, (7) ANAMNESIS, (8) offering, (9) EPIKLESIS, (10) intercessions, (11) DOXOLOGY.

Westminster Directory. The Directory for the Public Worship of God (1645), designed on Presbyterian principles to replace the *Book of Common Prayer*, composed by a commission of divines set up by parliament to report on a confession of faith, a form of ecclesiastical government, and forms of worship. The directory consists mostly of general instructions rather than forms of service.

White. The liturgical color used on feasts of Christ, the Virgin Mary, and saints who were not martyrs. It is often explained as suggesting purity and light.

Whitsunday (WIT-sun-day; Old English *hwita sunnandaeg*, white Sunday). The Day of Pentecost, the fiftieth day of Easter, so called from the custom of those baptized on the Vigil of Pentecost wearing white baptismal robes on this day.

Wimple (WIM-pul; Old English *wimpel*, something that winds around). A cloth wound around the head, framing the face, and gathered into folds beneath the chin, worn by women in the medieval period and as part of the habit of certain orders of nuns.

Wine, blessing of. See BLESSING OF WINE.

Winged rochet. See ROCHET.

Worship (Old English *weorthscipe* [worth-ship], honor, dignity, reverence). The adoration, love, and devotion rendered to one who is worthy of such honor. "Worship" is used without the indefinite article: one does not speak of "a worship." Worship is a general noun, not interchangeable with "service."

Worship service. An awkward and unpleasant phrase avoided by careful users of the English language, although common among sectarians. One properly speaks of "a service" or "a service of worship." Nouns are used to modify other nouns only when no appropriate adjective form is available. "Worship" is a noun, not an adjective; the adjectival form is "worshipful."

Worthy is Christ. A PROSE written for the *Lutheran Book of Worship* based on the DIGNUS EST AGNUS and Revelation 19:7-9; 5:9, 12-13; 15:2-4; 19:5-6; 5:11; 11:17, used as an alternative HYMN OF PRAISE in the ENTRANCE RITE of the Eucharist for the Fifty Days of Easter, Christ the King, and All Saints' Day.

Yy

Yom hashoah (YOHM ha-SHOW-ah; Hebrew, day of the holocaust). A remembrance of the Holocaust established in 1952 on the anniversary of the uprising in the Warsaw Ghetto in February 1943; the observance now takes place yearly in April. Although the day is primarily a Jewish memorial, it is observed by Christians in certain places.

Zeon (Greek, hot water). In the BYZANTINE RITE, a small metal container for hot water, poured into the chalice before the reception of Holy Communion.

Zoni (Greek, belt). The beltlike CINCTURE of the BYZANTINE RITE, worn to hold the priest's stole in place.

Zucchetto (zoo-KETT-o; Italian diminutive of *zucca*, head). A small round skullcap worn by certain Western Catholic clergy during mass, except during the CANON, and varying in color depending on the rank of the wearer (white for the pope, red for cardinals, violet for bishops, black for others). It was originally worn as a *submitrale* under the MITER to preserve it, covering the sides and back of the bishop's head; it was later much reduced in size.